Before I grow too old

PAT JILKS

INTRODUCTION

Everybody has something they would love to do.
Some ambitions are even legal. Mine was legal
and was a simple enough one. For years I had
wanted to walk from one end of Great Britain to
the other but, somehow, there had never been the
time.

Now, divorced late in life and with the children
gone away, I should have had the time but, as with so
many people, the care and responsibility for children was
to be replaced by that for an aged parent. In the case of
my sister and myself, it was Dad who had died and Mum
was unable to cope.

At first, it was difficult because we two sisters
lived at a distance from each other but finally, we looked at
each other and said, "Hey, this is a problem, but a problem
shared is a problem halved." So, we sold our houses,
bought a bigger one half-way between where we had both

been living before and the three of us moved in.

The nomadic spirit in me found it hard but, as time went on, we shuffled ourselves into a family unit. I still had this dream though and, although I certainly didn't want to dispatch Mum prematurely, I wondered who would go first – Mum or my knees. There was that old guy with a scythe too, who kept looking in my direction and sniggering.

Then, a very nice building society became a bank and gave me a chunk of money, for nothing, just for honouring them with my humble custom. That would give me the finance to do the walk and I began to get restless.

By this time we had seen that it was stupid for both of us to be totally bound by the caring and had settled into a month on/month off system, where each of us had a month in turn of total responsibility for hospital visits, shopping etc. and the next month could do our own thing. Mum never actually realised that we did this which was good because otherwise it might have made her feel like a job rather than our Mum. I did gardening and work in a vineyard when I could, which was flexible.

My sister thought I was a few stars short of a galaxy wanting to do such a long walk. She says that my passion is walking and hers is not walking, but she thought that I had better go off and do this walk before I exploded with frustration and a shower of bad tempered particles fell on everyone.

So, I earned myself a month's credit by doing an

extra 'caring' month and planned the walk to start the following year on 1ˢᵗ May.

Now, it was approaching that time. I had great fun planning the walk which I thought would take about two months and be around 1,200 miles long. I wasn't sure if Mum really understood what I was planning to do because her sense of geography was such that she wasn't really sure where East Grinstead was, or if she realised I would be away for so long. I hoped that she would be well when I was away.

A month before 1ˢᵗ May, everything seemed 'go' so, off I went to a travel agency to book a flight from Gatwick to Inverness.

"Only one way?" asked the girl behind the desk. "Aren't you coming back?"

"Yes, but I'm walking back," I replied.

The girl gave me a very hard stare. She obviously thought I was being sarcastic. She looked very young.

The cost for a one way ticket was twice what I expected but, unbelievably, a return ticket cost not much more than half, which was silly but caused me to decide to take a return and throw the other half away, which was even sillier.

The girl sniffed and gave me the ticket.

THE WALK

On 30th April, my sister drove me to Gatwick. It wasn't far, because we only live a short distance away. I thought that the plane looked a bit old but the wings seemed fixed on securely enough. I managed to get a window seat and the sky was a clear blue, without a cloud, so I'd be able to see down at the land, which was what I wanted.

A small child was screaming, which was a bit unnerving because I wondered whether it knew something that the rest of us didn't. It carried on screaming all the time we were waiting to start. I was going to be a grandmother for the first time in October. Surely, I should be having warm and grandmotherly feelings towards this small child, sympathetic at its fear, instead of wishing that someone would throttle the little mite but then, my grandchild will never behave like that!

We started off down the runway and the child stopped crying either because of the movement or being throttled. Then, we stood in a queue of airplanes for a while reminding me rather strongly of the M25, but we moved along, definitely faster than anything on the M25. Ahead, I could see a layer of black pollution in the London direction but we flew above it and I looked down. Wow! I could see footpaths all over the countryside. I must have walked along most of those at some time.

There was a town below and it looked as if there were quarries excavated all around it. Then, I realised that

they were not quarries, but building sites, lots of them.
There were so many building sites, cancelling out the fields
and countryside all around that town. It made me realise
how much is being built, all over our beautiful countryside.
The building seemed to stretch out like tendrils from every
nucleus of town and village and roads were everywhere,
cutting off chunks of countryside so that the first thing the
wild animals would have to learn nowadays is the green
cross code.

Looking down at that torn up mutilation, I felt
sorry for the earth. I wondered how does it feel when it
has been flattened and trapped underneath all those roads
and buildings? The earth seems to be losing its battle as
more of it is being crushed and smothered every year by
our civilisation and development and I wondered how
long it would be before the concrete had won. When this
planet is all covered, perhaps we can find another one that
is still green - heck, there are enough of them out there to
choose from. But still, it is sad.

Now I could see a huge town ahead. I could
recognise the pattern of bends in the river. London!
Looking down, I actually saw the park and lakes along
which my daughter and I had walked only two days before.
That was a strange feeling.

I could see the two engines of the plane out of the
window, but not the stuff coming out of them that was
pushing us along and which makes the lines up in the sky.
I was sitting in a metal bird, loaded with such heaviness,
yet flying! It gave me a sense of lightness and freedom
being up high in the sky like that and I could imagine

myself floating out and soaring over the landscape.

To keep us all happy and occupied, we were given breakfast. I smiled at the lady sitting next to me. She fixed me for a moment with a cold unsmiling stare and turned away. "I'm not going to encourage this person to talk to me," said her expression, but it was the last thing I wanted to do anyway. There was too much to look at out of the window.

Now there were rigid shapes of fields below us, so many of them in bright yellow. There must be a good subsidy on oil seed rape this year but do we really need all that? I remembered an interesting heading in Farmer's Weekly once that announced, 'Rape popular with farmers this year.'

The lady next to me was smart and sophisticated, reading an upmarket magazine. Next to her sat a less sophisticated person who thought it was all marvellous, with face pressed up to the window. A bird passing outside would just see two wide open eyes and a flattened nose. It was not 'cool' behaviour at all.

Below, it began to get very hilly and I thought we were probably flying over the Pennines. You couldn't really see how high the hills were from up in the plane, but the type of vegetation changed with height from looking bright green and cultivated to a duller green and rougher. Sometimes there were very dark patches of forest. It got even wilder down there and now, there was snow on the hills. The pilot told us that we had reached Scotland. Well, that didn't take long, but it would take a lot longer to walk back

I saw some lakes below that might be reservoirs because they were completely straight across at one end and I wondered if that was natural or artificial.

I could actually see where the top bit of Scotland had, long ago, taken a trip across the sea to smash into the rest of the UK. I could see too, on the hills, the grooves and gouges where glaciers in the past had raked the mountains like a giant emery board. What a sight that would have been – glaciers and snow cliffs everywhere, blue and sparkling in the sun, with just the occasional mammoth stuck in a crevice.

After what seemed such a short while, we arrived at Inverness. Outside, there was a young lady hailing a taxi. "Want to share?" I asked, so we did. She was from Kent, wearing a fur coat because she was sure it would be cold up here, but today it was not cold at all, but sunny and warm.

The taxi driver told me that it would be better to take a bus to Wick rather than the train, because the train goes all the way around inland and takes a couple of hours longer than the bus to get there.

While the taxi was waiting at traffic lights in Inverness, he related, with suitable hand movements, how a few days earlier, at that very spot, he had spied a movement out of the corner of his eye. When he looked to see what it was, there was a huge spider scuttling across the road, bigger than any he had ever seen before.

"An escaped tarantula that had been a pet?" I enquired hopefully because, if it had been an escaped pet, there would only have been one of them and so less chance of meeting it.

"No Just an ordinary spider, but enormous," he said.

I didn't really want to hear that. If it was just an ordinary spider, there could be lots of them. I am not afraid of snakes, frogs, mice, rats, beetles, crane-flies or politicians, but spiders now, they give me the shakes. I shall be sleeping out at times and Dounreay Power Station is not far away. Could it be that large mutated spiders are lying in wait for a warm sleeping bag to give them comfort for the night?

I caught a bus to Wick and then another to John O'Groats. The main road up the coast that the bus travelled on looked lethal to walkers, but I'd decided not to walk on main roads unless I had to. The bus driver said that, up until now, it had been really misty and you couldn't see far, so how lucky I was that it was clear. Even if it rained tomorrow, the countryside had welcomed me and shown itself with a smiling face.

When I got off the bus, two delightful children, one with a mountain bike so covered in mud that I thought he was riding a manure heap, showed me where my B & B was. It is often a bit of an ordeal to walk past a group of children in England if you are grey haired, with glasses and wearing a large rucksack, especially in or near towns. I have found that, more often or not, they snigger as I pass and shout out humourless and somewhat spiteful quips, often of a sexual nature and I have come to expect this sort of treatment and steel myself for it but here, the children were not like that at all. I got a lovely welcome at Skona View and left my rucksack to walk to the most easterly point of the British Isles.

I looked out to sea, and there was a surprise. I had expected to be looking far, far away, across an endless expanse of sea, feeling that I was right on the edge of the land, but it didn't feel like the edge at all, because there were islands out there in front of me. I stood under a blue sky and the islands floating on the sea looked like they were from a fairytale of ancient times.

The largest island was (and still is) Orkney. I had heard that there were structures on these islands, pretty intact, where people lived 5,000 years ago. Imagine that! All those years ago, there were people up here, but no roads and tracks to anywhere else much. Where I had just come from in so few hours would have seemed like a journey to a foreign country. I expect that they would have travelled by sea rather than land.

Seeing those islands out there made me want to go further on and explore them all. I wondered why the people had chosen to live on an island that must have been more exposed than some parts of the mainland and if it was because they would have been safer there. When you could see the sea all around, perhaps it was more likely that you could notice if you were being crept up on by invaders and easier to repel them. If you had enough water, fish, crops and animals, that was pretty well all you needed.

Tempting though it was to visit the islands, I thought that if I allowed myself to indulge in too many diversions, I'd never get on with the walk, so decided to leave that pleasure to another time. One day, I would come up here again and visit all those beautiful islands, giving them the time and attention they deserved, instead of rushing it. Now, they looked beautiful indeed, basking under a blue sky and warm sun, but I could imagine how they could change in looks with the weather. Never boring though.

I knew that there was a sign here at the 'end' pointing in different directions and giving the mileage to all sorts of places. I had intended to take a photo to prove I'd been there but It had an addition on it that said "Well done, you've made it!" which was not really applicable, as I hadn't even started yet.

It seemed obvious that the world is expected to start from Lands End and end at John O'Groats and here I was, all set to start walking the other way. I had considered this seriously. It did, indeed, make much more sense to start at Lands End. There is more civilisation there while a person got used to walking. By the time they got to the less inhabited regions, they would be hardened up or dead. Also, the wind direction and the sun would be mostly behind the person that way. This way, I would be walking against the wind and looking into the sun.

All this I knew, but decided all the same to walk from the top down. It was just how I wanted to do it and psychologically, I'd be walking towards home, even if I was going to overshoot it by many miles. Also, I would be walking in Scotland before the famous midges and small things start biting.

I should have liked £1 for every person who joked

to me (I think they were joking), "Oh, you'll be walking downhill all the way." I should also like another £1 for every one of those who were totally wrong about that.

Such a beautiful day to be at the top of Scotland, but there was nobody else here at all. I'd somehow expected there to be tourists, but I was alone, which was rather nice. There was a phone box so I phoned home to the family to boast of where I was. It was amazing that I had started from Gatwick at 9.30 and arrived at my destination before 6.

The sun was setting and I took off my glasses to watch it because I am short sighted and without my glasses on, it looked even more beautiful. I swear that the impressionist artists were all short sighted, because that is how I see the world without aid and I can see close to me perfectly well to read, or to paint what I see, if I was so gifted. Colours seem brighter and merge beautifully without the specs on.

I knew that nights would be very short during the whole of my walk. That was another reason I wanted to start on 1st May. Right at the top here, they were even shorter, because it is nearer the North Pole. If I was going to have to sleep out, then the shorter the night the better. Also though, because it is so near the North Pole, I was right underneath the ozone hole. In the south, we are protected a bit from the ultra-violet by the pollution, but here, there is no pollution, so I realised I must be very careful not to get burned because, even with cloud cover, the danger was there.

I'd thought I would be too anxious and excited

about starting the walk to sleep that night, but I hardly remember trying and woke up to the first day of the longest walk of my life.

* * *

Last night was the only place I had booked in advance. Now, I was to take my chance. It would have been such a stress booking ahead and having to be in a certain place by a fixed date and time. It didn't allow for one of my specialities – getting lost. I knew that, this way would be sometimes difficult, but preferred that rather than having a schedule to keep to.

The first question people always seemed to ask about the walk was "Are you doing the walk for charity?" Well, I wasn't. I was doing the walk just for the hell of it. The fuss of getting it all organised and people to sponsor me was more than I could stand the thought of. Mean though it might be – for this walk, I wanted to be free! If I were doing it for charity, I would have had to be responsible to that organisation but, by myself, if for any reason – and there was always the possibility that Mum would become ill and I would have to give up the walk - I would not be letting anybody else down.

For the times when I would have to sleep out I had brought a waterproof bivvy bag, lightweight sleeping bag and a sleeping mat that had little cells which self-inflate when you open a valve. I'm not daft though. I like comfort and, if I could get it in the form of accommodation, I was going to do so, but taking sleeping equipment with me meant that, when I couldn't find anywhere to stay, then I should survive.

Of course, if the weather supplied warm, balmy and dry nights, it might even be a pleasure to sleep outside and I would choose that, saving a lot of money in the process, but sad experience of nights spent out in this manner tell me the truth. In our country, those comfortable nights are very rare. It is much more often cold, or wet, or both. My body doesn't carry enough spare fat to keep me very warm, or cover bones that seem to dig in everywhere in a most uncomfortable manner. Sleeping out just happens to be the only way to do the walks I really want to do and discomfort at night is worth the pleasures of the day.

Walking along, I saw how very flat it was up here. I wasn't expecting that. I had never been to Scotland before and somehow thought all of it would be hilly, but this part was like a pancake, with some fields but, more often, moorland.

I passed Canisbay, walking towards Slickly. The road was very straight and stretched ahead of me on and on, across a moor. The weather was brilliant that day, with lots of sun, but quite a chilly wind, so not comfortable to sit down for long. It was very remote there, with nothing much except the moor surrounding me and I loved it. Sometimes I dream of walking a road like this, that stretches ahead as far as I can see and now, here I was, walking my dream. Mountains were ahead of me, way in the distance and it was quiet – oh how quiet. There were no planes, no traffic, no people, only birds - Magic.

Places were marked on the map that I had assumed would be settlements of a group of houses, but they turned out to be only one or two buildings. I suppose the map compilers got a bit desperate to find something other than clumps of heather to put on their map.

The farms and cultivated land I passed did not

look very prosperous or fertile. It seemed to be a hard sort of way to make a living up at the top there and probably always had been.

I walked about 11 miles and was dying for a 'cuppa'. I could have made myself one, but it was a fiddly business. Also, Lyth Arts Centre was marked on the map and two girls with horses said that they sold teas there so, even though it was a bit off my route, I scuttled along eagerly. I had an idea in my head of the Arts Centre being sort of 'twee', selling crafts and arty objects, like they often are in Sussex, but here, there was nobody much around to sell anything to and this was a real arts centre, with a theatre.

There was nobody in sight and the place looked as though it was shut. I knocked at the door and a gentleman opened it. No, he said, they did not open for teas until later in the season. It was too early yet.

My mouth turned down and I felt grumpy, as the bubble above my head, which had been featuring a nice cup of tea, burst with a despondent slurp. Then, the most lovely gentleman who had answered my enquiring knock said, "Come in anyway. I'll give you some tea." And he did.

I sat in the kitchen with him and another gentleman and they gave me home-made scones and a big pot of tea. I drank three cups, straight off, without blinking.

They looked at my map and told me of a better route than I'd planned through the woods the next day.

It's lonely out there, they said, desolate and a bit sad now, because no longer populated, but beautiful. The lodges, which look more like castles and are a bit 'over the top' were built in Victorian times for the gentry to use when on hunting trips and that was when the railway was diverted to go that way, not for the benefit of the ordinary people, but for the ones that used the hunting lodges. Now, those lodges are not used very much.

The gentleman who first welcomed me said that, when he was a child, his mother used to teach in a little school out there. Her class comprised of seven children, belonging to the railway man and forester. It was a very lonely life, he said.

I set off refreshed but, after a few more miles, my hips started to hurt – getting used to the hip belt and weight of the rucksack. After all, it was only the first day, so I started to look for somewhere to sleep.

The cold wind made me wish to be sheltered during the night and not out on the open moor. After a while, I saw just the place. It was a small copse of woodland with a wall on one side of it that would act as a good shelter. The ground was flat and firm there, with no brambles and soft from the leaves and needles fallen on it.

As I went into the copse, there was an almighty kerfuffle and noise. It was a rookery, with a large population of birds and much fuss was being made of this intrusion into their domain but soon, they saw that I was harmless and accepted my presence. I carefully chose a place that was not below a lot of nests, as I didn't want to have a layer of white all over my bivvy by morning.

I set out my gear and made a hot drink. My 'stove' was just a thin bit of metal, which opened up like Tower Bridge. On top, I could balance my enamel mug of water. Underneath, I placed quarter of a lighted fuel block. I found that the blocks were easy to light, especially since I brought extra long matches, so easy in fact that at first; I burned my fingers a bit, because the flames were not very visible. I put a piece of aluminium foil on top of the mug to keep in the heat and placed another piece on the bottom under the fuel block, so that there was no danger of setting anything alight. I found that, just over a quarter of a block heated the water, if it was out of the wind.

My daughter had insisted that I take this piece of equipment so that I could have a hot drink and I had not wanted to take it.

"Its extra weight," I said. "I'm, trying to cut down as much as possible on weight and I've never bothered with such a luxury before."

"Not a luxury," said daughter. "A life saver."

She had just come back from walking in the Himalayas, the hard way, without a guide, so she did know what she was talking about.

"But it's not the Himalayas, its Scotland," I said.

"Hypothermia," she replied firmly. "Comes on you without you hardly knowing," and, to settle the argument, she bought me a stove and fuel blocks and gave them to me accompanied by a very hard stare and in a manner which did not allow for any dispute. Now, enjoying a warming drink, I accepted that it had been a good idea.

I snuggled down in my sleeping bag, with all my clothes on, because it was pretty nippy. It was lovely looking up at the branches above me, black against the sky, getting more and more indistinct as the sky darkened. It was cloudy and cold but not quite raining.

The rooks were settling down too, with an unbelievable fuss and noise, but this finally subsided into friendly chats, then just a muttering.

Do you know that rooks talk in their sleep? Not many people know that, but they do. All night. And sometimes, it sounds as if one has fallen off its branch, accompanied by such a flapping and squawking for a while.

Plop!

"Squawk!" Flap.

"Caw-w-w. Wotzat?"

"Oh, it's only Bert, fallen off his bloody perch again. Caww-z-z-z."

There were lots of other, smaller plops too. I was grateful that I had placed myself under an uninhabited tree.

It was very cold that night, so I just dozed and, as soon as the daylight came, jumped about a bit and had breakfast, which consisted of Scots oat-cakes and dates. I chose the oat-cakes because they were nourishing, filled me up and also were extremely boring and unappetising when eaten by themselves so that I knew I would only eat what I needed to stop being hungry. Less eaten, the less there is to carry. The dates got a bit boring too after a couple of days, but it was all good fuel, to keep the poor old body going.

It was pretty early when I passed through Watten, but there was an open door with a man going in, so I asked him if he would kindly fill up my water bottle, which he did with a bit of a surprised look, but a smile. That is one advantage of being a grey-haired old biddy. People in general, especially other women, do not feel threatened or intimidated by me and I get the bottle filled with a smile and sometimes a nice chat too.

Westerdale was where a track branched off to Strathmore Lodge. There was a phone box there, so I rang my daughter. As I was talking to her – clunk – the right lens fell clean out of my specs. Luckily the lens was made of plastic, but it was a bit of a surprise. Then, I saw with the remaining lens, that three chickens were pecking eagerly at my rucksack. I terminated the conversation rather rapidly, gathered up the fallen lens, chased off the chickens and put on my sunglass specs. They were prescription sunglasses because, otherwise, I wouldn't have been able to see much further than my own nose, but it felt really stupid wearing dark glasses, as the weather was dull and overcast to begin with and now, wearing the sunglasses, everything looked very gloomy indeed.

After a time of walking down the track, I found a

good place to sit for a while and stuck the lens back into my glasses in a most artistic manner, with little bits of sticking plaster. I thought they looked very fetching – designer specs. I could see there was a possibility of the fashion catching on but, more importantly, I could see the world in a much brighter light..

A lady and gentleman cycled by and stopped, at which point, the man fell over, together with his bike. This was unexpected and impressive, but he explained that he had new toe-clips on the pedals that he wasn't used to yet and couldn't get his feet out in time. Luckily, he wasn't hurt and we had a very nice chat. Such friendly people make for pleasant encounters and I learn a lot about the area I am walking.

Now, my way was through forests that were very different from what I had expected. Somehow, I'd thought the woods and forest up here would be like they are at home, with solid ground underneath, where I could sit a while and sleep if necessary, but it was not like that at all. These trees were not growing in solid ground, they grew in bog! It was not level ground either, but consisted of tussocks and mounds of moss, with that ankle-twisting bog in

between. There was nowhere flat to place a waterproof bivvy bag because, if a person did do that and lay down on it, that person would probably sink without trace.

Even if the ground were not so wet, it was pretty impossible to get in amongst the trees anyway – not here. There were often high fences each side of the track, either keeping the deer in or out, I supposed. Even when there was a section without fences, the bog and thick scrub bordering the edges made it extremely difficult to get into the woods.

This was a bit of a shame, because I love going a little way into woods and sitting quietly under the trees for a while. I often do this at home. When you sit there without moving, the creatures come out. Once, when I was sitting in some woods like this, I saw a movement to my side and there, within touching distance, was a mouse, climbing up a foxglove. It had a very long tail and broke off a foxglove seed with its little paws, put it in its mouth to carry and scuttled down the stem. It was just like a picture in a fairytale story book.

I began to think of stopping because I'd walked quite a way by now and was beginning to tire. There was nowhere I could stop comfortably though, so I carried on, taking the way the gentleman at the arts centre had told me, which cut off quite a distance that I would otherwise have walked. Altnabreac station was my destination.

By the time I got to the station, which was really small, I was pretty tired and it had started to rain. There was a hut nearby and I looked inside to see if there was room for a person to sleep there, but there were just boards, with lots of bird shit on them and goodness knows what else shit. The boards had big gaps and, looking down, there was a pool of rancid and murky water below. No! Definitely not for sleeping, but as I turned to go out, my map slipped from my fingers and fell down into the water. For a moment, I panicked, because without my map I'm lost – literally.

Now, people find this difficult to believe because I go walking a lot, but I have absolutely no sense of direction whatsoever. However, I can read a compass and map reasonably well so, that's how I find my way. The compass is hanging around my neck all the time like a positive albatross and the page of the map I want is inside a plastic sleeve and tucked in the hip-belt of my rucksack.

Fortunately, on this occasion, I had something with me that saved me from a nasty get-lost experience. It was an umbrella. A very cheap umbrella, but long as a walking stick. I had seen on the TV that many walkers seemed to take an umbrella with them, so thought I'd try it. I didn't really need a walking stick on these small roads and tracks, so the umbrella was carried in the rucksack belt crossways. I wasn't sure about its worth yet, but now it earned its transportation so far by being used to hook up the map from the water. I found that it was only a bit wet inside the plastic and felt very happy and relieved to get it back.

There was a small hut-type waiting room at the station and a house nearby. I knocked at the house to see if it was all right to stop there, but nobody answered, so I set up home inside the hut anyway. I was very pleased to be inside as it was raining really hard by now.

I consulted the menu. "Oat-cake and dates", it said there. It had an alternative – "Dates and oat-cake". I made a careful decision and chose the former. After my meal, I settled into my sleeping bag. I didn't drink anything all evening, hoping that it meant I didn't have to get out of my sleeping bag during the night and go outside in the cold and rain. That is such a performance, getting out of the bag and in again.

It was very cold, much colder than the night before. I dozed a bit, then suddenly, I was wide awake. My daughter was lying at the bottom of my sleeping bag, curled up asleep, and I was very worried that she was getting too cold. I could see the shape of her curled up there, but as I reached out, realised that I was hallucinating.

I knew that hallucinations could be one of the first signs of hypothermia setting in. I had felt cold all right but shouldn't have thought it was bad enough for hypothermia. I did have a survival sheet of foil with me, but you sweat so much in this, so would rather only use it when it's a matter of life or death. Now, I changed things by getting up, jumping around for a bit and making myself a hot drink.

I mentally thanked my daughter for making me bring this little stove and being part of a warning hallucination.

After this, I felt fine and drifted off to sleep now and again until it was daylight.

There was a lot of lovely wet moss around, so I used this as a sort of damp sponge to wash with. I got a lot of bits all over me, some of which didn't bear too close an examination, but felt very refreshed and clean. I don't like feeling dirty from not washing, so use what is around. Dew is always good.

In the morning, the weather was not too bad, sort of rainy but not being very serious about it. I started walking along the railway line. The trains here were diesel, not electric. I intended to come off the line as soon as I could if there was a path, but there didn't seem to be one, it looked pretty thick vegetation all around and there were high fences each side of the track, so I didn't have any choice about walking on the line as I couldn't get out anyway.

I carried on walking, in such silence, that I knew I would hear any trains coming easily. It was desolate all around, very misty and mysterious. I stopped often, just to listen to the silence. Even the bird sounds were muted in the mist.

The walking was hard along the track. If I walked at the side, it was very uneven and all chips of granite, so I usually chose to walk along the sleepers, but soon found that the slats of wood were not placed in a very thoughtful way for walkers. Sometimes they were too close together, so that I walked like Charlie Chaplin, then they jumped to giant strides and I was like a woman walking on the moon. I must have looked like a strange sort of walker, taking little mincing steps and then suddenly striding wide.

Once, a train came by. I heard it coming when it was a long way off and stood still, as far away from the track as possible, trying to look innocent, as though I was just casually standing there - on the wrong side of a 6 ft high fence. "What me trespassing? Never! I'm just standing here, in the middle of nowhere, admiring the view." As the train passed, the driver gave me a toot.

Oh well, I couldn't get off anyway, although I was quite happy with this new experience. About every mile, there was a railway hut, for line workers I suppose, so I could stop and go inside one to shelter when I wanted and make myself a hot drink. This was luxury.

I supposed it was about 9 miles along the track, although it seemed like longer. Then, I came to Forsinard. There was a visitor centre there at the station, with a very good bird display and a video of the birds actually nesting out on the moor, so I stayed for a while, in comfort.

Then, I walked down the road, heading for Kinbrace. I had read a book that reported a shop and B & B there. I had not been looking forward to walking this section on a mainish road, but needn't have worried, because if two cars came together within 10 minutes of each other, you could assume they were friends. I could hardly believe that this road was so nearly free of traffic, which was pleasure enough but added to that was the comfort of walking on a flat surface after the hard going on the railway track.

Before I started this walk, I had had to decide whether it was going to be done mainly on footpaths, or on small roads and tracks, because it had to be one or the other. Footwear would differ and I couldn't afford to carry the weight of different types of boot and shoe. Walking boots are totally unsuitable for roads, they jolt the leg too much and cause stress on the shins. Trainers are great on the hard surfaces because they have cushioned soles and bounce along, but they do slip more on rough ground and are not waterproof. I knew I'd need to take a spare pair of trainers in case of trouble with the main footwear. That could happen in the middle of nowhere.

On investigation, I found that, if I took footpaths, it would take me much longer to walk the distance and I'd have to carry much larger-scale walking maps. I would either have to carry a big and heavy pile of these or buy them along the way, which would not be easy as I may not be anywhere near suitable shops. For walking on small roads and tracks, I just needed 34 pages, torn from Phillips Navigator Road Map and weighing a mere one pound in total. So that was what I opted for.

It made for a completely different type of walk than any I'd done before, but which I thought would be very interesting, as it would take me through villages and small towns, where I could talk to people and see how life was lived in different parts of the UK. It would give me a real taste into, not just the scenery, but the dynamics of my own country.

My decision was that I bought a new pair of bouncy trainers with ankle support, one size too big, which meant I could wear two pairs of socks for further cushioning against the pounding of feet on hard tarmac. I had a dear, old, faithful and battered pair of trainers which I got resoled as an extra pair. So far, the new trainers were very comfortable and no trouble at all.

I had reached the hills now and walked along the road with moors and lakes to each side of me and mountains not far away. One of the mountains looked just like a volcano, with an indented cone. Above it was a cloud that made it look like smoke was coming out of it, which added to the illusion.

Sitting down for a while, I thought about how it must have looked here, where I was sitting, millions and millions of years ago. In those times, all these worn down hills would have been active volcanoes, spewing out fire and smoke. If we could see a fast forward video of the British Isles over these aeons of time, we would see parts of the land surface going up and down like a yo-yo as, in turn, it was under the sea, shallow lakes, desolation, sand dunes, forest, desert, green land – always changing, nothing staying the same forever.

Once, when my son was about 5 years old, I tried to transmit this impressive information of how the landscape had changed.

"Do you know," I said, "That millions of years ago, where we are walking now was once under water."

"Oh," replied he, looking at the vegetation dripping from a recent shower of rain.

"That's why it's so wet then."

It seems to be general, though, that alteration of what has been perceived to be the 'norm' is resented. People look at the scenery and get very rattled and annoyed when any change starts taking place in it, but everything changes, all the time. Its not that you can't try to make the changes good ones instead of bad, but change it will, whether we like it or not.

Sitting there and realising that this constant

fluidity and change is a natural structure of the whole planet made me sorry that so many of us humans don't understand that. We are forever trying to hold on to things in our lives as they have been in the past, not accepting that, whether we like it nor not, nothing stays the same. We cause ourselves a lot of unhappiness in this way – clinging and clutching to the safe familiar, instead of seeing change as opportunity and excitement.

I have these deep philosophical thoughts when I'm walking like this and always make a mental decision to change my way of thinking or behaviour accordingly, but usually fail miserably within a short while of returning home. It is one good reason why I'm always having to go off on walks. To remind myself!

The railway was parallel to the road and a train went by. As he passed, the driver gave me a toot. It must have been the same driver who passed me on the track. There were not many trains, so it might well be.

By the time I got to Kinbrace, I was very tired. The first part of the day had been hard along the rails and I found the rucksack had got much heavier as the day went on. My shoulders hurt.

I looked hopefully for the shop and B & B mentioned in the book I had read. I walked up and down but saw no shop. I asked some gentlemen at a workshop and learned that it had been closed a while back. I couldn't see a B & B either and knocked on a door to ask where it was. A lady answered and pointed out where it should be, but she was not sure if they still did it. She said, if they didn't, she would give me a bed for the night, which was really kind.

At the house I was directed to, the lady there said she didn't do B & B at the moment, because she had to go off to work early, but looked at me, smiled and said, if I didn't mind that they were not really ready for visitors and was willing to have breakfast early, then she would take me.

I was very appreciative of this and determined to try and disrupt them as little as possible. I reassured her that I had enough food for myself that evening, which I did, boring though it was. I'd saved myself a little treat of choc bar and sesame seed biscuits. I had a hot bath and felt very content, because I could make as much tea as I wanted. That was all I needed to be very happy.

The lovely couple were very kind and concerned for my future welfare. They telephoned ahead to a B & B they knew which was just past Lothbeg for the next night. They had two beautiful dogs, one of which reminded me of our own dog Poppy, who is still on the farm and greets me with the heart of a puppy when I go there, even though she has the body of an old dog now.

Later, I walked down the road to tell the lady who offered me a bed that I was OK and to thank her very much for her offer. I felt warmed by the kindness of the people there.

I felt much refreshed in the morning after my good rest and it was great to know I had a place to stay that night and a meal there too. Proper food!

I noticed that the road I was walking on now called itself an 'A' road, but had even less traffic than the day before. I sat for a while, enjoying the beauty of the moors around me and listening to the many different bird sounds. Then, to my left, I heard a strange sounding deep warble, loud and long. This was followed immediately by another warble, then another, another and yet another, warbling in turn, all around me.

I seemed to be sitting inside a circle of warblers, not all calling together, but one after another. It was very puzzling. Perhaps it was one bird flying from place to place, but I looked carefully and saw no sign of movement at all.

Why? What? I thought hard about it.

Perhaps there was only one bird, which was a ventriloquist.

Then again, maybe there were several of them, warbling clockwise. Either I had sat by chance in the middle of a committee meeting, or they had been waiting all their lives for someone to sit in that particular place so that they could do this.

Ah - There was a network of tunnels, with holes at intervals and the one bird warbles, then runs like hell down the tunnel, popping its head up to warble at the next place, and so on.

Or, it could be that a bird has encountered a group of Klingons from Star Trek, managed to get hold of one of their Klingon Cloaking Devices and has made itself invisible.

I thought that the last explanation was probably the most likely.

I left the birds to their lonely warbling and cut off at Kildonan Lodge, down a very small road. I didn't encounter another soul while walking among tussocks, heather and rushing streams, with high hills all around.

I looked up at the high ridges which towered above me and there, on my right, silhouetted all along the ridge, were the Apaches, lined up and waiting to swoop down on me, after my scalp. Then, to my relief, I saw that they were not Indians at all, but deer, a large herd of them, watching me warily.

I heard a cuckoo. I'd heard one yesterday, for the first time.

"What a shame dear, that most of our babies this year fell out of the nest, but junior here is going to be a strapping big bird, by the size of him now."

And the amazing thing about cuckoos is how they get it all together, without being told, because each one is in isolation and has never seen its parents or another cuckoo. Yet, at a certain time (and this is after the parents have gone flying off, so they get no help there), all the young cuckoos get together – at the same time – and fly off abroad.

What on earth told them to do this? How did they know when and where to gather? How did they know where to fly? It's like some pre-programmed software is switched on inside their little heads, maybe triggered into action by the length of a certain day. Little computers in flight. Who can tell?

* * *

I joined the main coast road. After the beautiful and deserted track I had been on, walking on, this busy and hazardous road came as a nasty shock. I trudged along it a bit wearily and it seemed a long way to the B & B.   On the way I saw a stone at the side of the road, which was inscribed:

To mark the place near which

(According to Scrope's "Art of Deerstalking")

The last wolf in Sutherland

was killed

by the hunter Polson

in or about the year 1700

This stone was erected by

His Grace the Duke of Portland,K.C.,

A.D. 1924

I couldn't help feeling sorry for this last, poor, bewildered and lonely wolf, wandering without a pack (or a rucksack), howling at the moon.

Now, I hear, it is planned to reintroduce the wolf to the Highlands. I have heard the sheep muttering about it in a worried fashion.

I got to my destination finally and was greeted with a lovely welcome and a meal! Again, there was kind concern for my welfare and a phone call to a B & B at

Golspie, where I intended to stop next.

Mrs D. put my trousers and T-shirt into the washing machine and, as it was a bit cold for shorts, loaned me track suit bottoms to go down to the beach. This was just across the railway and a couple of fields so, off I went. I felt great, walking on the sand barefooted. There were so many different kinds of rocks here, some of them volcanic. Mr and Mrs D. had found many tiny ammonites on this beach and I searched diligently, but without luck.

Scotland seemed to be a marvellous place for looking at rocks and I loved thinking about how it must have been, long ago. Once, there were lots of little ammonites, swimming in the sea and bigger ones too, together with many other strange looking creatures, but we'll never know what most of them looked like. I have read that more than 98% of all living species that have inhabited the earth throughout time, have become extinct. That was before we started on them, wiping them out systematically.

There is a fantastic variety of creatures inhabiting the earth now, but this is such a small part of what has been wandering or swimming around in the past. We can only piece together what we suppose is the history of the earth, from the small bits we find here and there. One day, when the human species is also extinct, in its turn, visitors from another planet might arrive and try to piece together the past from what they find.

You will see

Here is an example of one

enclosed in its metal shell.

Damaged somewhat,

possibly by collision with another.

Which seemed to happen often

and we think may have been a

contribution to their extinction.

Although there are many other theories.

The birds here were not afraid of me. They flew very close.

On my return, to the welcome of hens, ducks and four lovely dogs, I found that my trousers were already dry. I bought these ones especially for this sort of thing because they dry within 15 minutes after a good soaking, so it was not really necessary to wear waterproof ones. I had brought some very light waterproof trousers though, mainly for extra warmth.

I had decided on what clothing to bring with me from past experience.

Three T-shirts, one for wearing, one probably damp in process of drying after washing and one spare.

Two silk shirts, purchased at charity shops. Silk is great because it weighs very little, squashes up small for packing and dries quickly. It is both warm and cool. I wear one of these shirts to protect my arms from the sun or for extra warmth, with the other kept clean for wearing when at a B & B. A pair of shorts, mostly for wearing while I wash my trousers. Four pairs of brief briefs.. A sleeveless fleece, which is terrific and cushions my shoulders a bit from the rucksack. A very light coat rather than a sweater, because it's lighter in weight and more windproof. A light waterproof coat, sun hat and woolly hat for keeping my head warm when I sleep out – it makes a lot of difference. Finally, two pairs of 'thousand mile' socks, which have two layers, so the material rubs over more material and not the foot. It works, because I don't get blisters, not even when walking in wet shoes. I had bought trainers a size too big and wore a pair of the thousand mile socks and another pair over the top, so carried two pairs of these top socks too. That was the clothes total. They didn't weigh that much to carry, because usually, in the British climate, I was wearing most of them.

Pansies were smiling at me from a window box outside my bedroom window. To one side, I could see a view of the beach and sea through pine trees and, on the other side, were the hills.

Next morning, I started walking along the beach towards Brora. The sun was shining on the sea, making it sparkle and patterning the yellow sand were the rocks of different shapes and colours.

I came to a stream, gushing out from the land

down to the sea and managed to cross that one, but soon came to another, which was much too wide and deep, so had to leave the beach to get around it.

I came to Brora and looked hopefully for a tea room. They were there, but none of them were open. Apparently, it was a bit early in the season, which highlighted how short the tourist season is up here.

Now, I had to walk on the busy main road again. There was a bit of a verge that I could stumble along, but a huge vehicle came rushing by and the wind it created by its passing almost knocked me off my feet. I only kept myself upright by clinging onto a post and felt very unnerved.

When, soon after, I stopped in safety a short way down a track, I found that my woolly hat had been blown off without me noticing. It was bright red, but I couldn't see it. I met a lady on a bike, who was wearing a most beautiful turquoise shirt. Co-incidentally, she worked with the lady who ran the B & B house I was heading for so she said, if she found my hat, she would bring it around that evening.

I had noticed from the map that Dunrobin Castle was just before Golspie and I'd planned to have a short walking day and visit it. I walked down the drive and there it was, a beautiful castle and grounds, not to mention in possession of very nice tea-rooms, which I welcomed with great enthusiasm and visited before doing anything else.

There was a display of predatory birds in the grounds of the Castle that day. A man told us about the different birds and let them fly to show us their skills.

There were owls of different kinds, on perches. I thought that owls all went to sleep in the day, but he said most do not and, indeed, these ones were wide awake, fixing us with their big eyes and twisting their heads round in exorcist style. He said that the neck bones are only as thick as your finger, so this is why they can rotate their heads like that. Mostly, the owls are all feathers, with little substance underneath. I thought, rather uncharitably, that this description would fit some types of very important people – all fluffed up feathers, with little substance underneath.

A tawny owl flew from behind us to get the food the man offered and then, a snowy owl swept in, so low and close to my left ear that I thought the ear was going with it. Then he let some of us wear the glove and have an owl settle. Thus, I found myself gazing in wonder at a beautiful snowy owl perched on my hand, regarding me with great wisdom (or did I see a bit of scorn in its gaze?)

The trainer showed how the falcon flies, sailing to a great height, so that it can get a really fast downward swoop to take food while on the wing. He twirled a bit of food very fast above his head. The falcon flew up high, then zoom! A flash of feathers going fast and the food had gone. He said they need much energy for this way of hunting, so eat a lot, but the hawk catches its prey on the ground and lands to eat it. He flew the hawk too and showed how it ripped its 'prey' to pieces.

There was a museum there, which had many interesting exhibits. One was an Egyptian mummy case. The mummy that had been found in it had an extra vertebra, said the notice. Wow! Just like me. I've got an extra bone too, which has been giving me some pain, because extra bones don't like the strain of a rucksack pulling on them. I always thought that having it must have been the result of having had polio when I was very young. I got off lucky with that disease, only having a strangely balanced backbone to show for it and, (I assumed,) the spare bone. Maybe though, I have an Egyptian ancestor somewhere back down the line. I am a mummy and perhaps – the nose….

I left Dunrobin, and arrived in Golspie in time to get the lens fitted back in my glasses. The optician was very impressed by my sticking plaster repairs and said I was the second person from my part of Sussex to come in that day with a fallen-out lens. I didn't think I'd better say that perhaps there are a lot of bad screws in Sussex, so just kept quiet. He wouldn't charge me anything, so I put some money into the charity box.

The optician was typical of what I was discovering about the people up here. They are so generous and giving, yet life is really hard for most of them. There didn't seem to be much work, the tourist season is very short, farming is a tough life, yet its expensive to live because everything has to be transported a long distance. Diesel fuel gets more expensive each year, with extra taxes put on it and such-like, so everything they buy gets more expensive too.

The only thing really cheap, is property. You can't sell it easily. Many places I passed were in ruins and quite a few shops in Golspie were shut down, yet everywhere it was so clean, no litter or graffiti on the walls like at home.

So, it seemed that people here have a tough time, yet are kind and proud of the environment. What does that say? I couldn't help comparing the poverty, yet dignity here with the easier life, yet lots of whining, that there is down south. Like spoilt kids?

Overlooking Golspie, on the top of Ben Bhraggie, was a statue of the 1st Duke of Sutherland. Apparently, he made many improvements in the area, but also cruelly threw out thousands of people from their small and humble dwellings in the Sutherland Glens to put sheep there, so he's not particularly remembered with love. He did die though, in 1833. That seems to happen with monotonous regularity, however rich you are.

The hat did not return, so somewhere in the Highlands, there is probably a sheep proudly wearing a red woolly hat and telling all her friends that it comes from a far off land, where all the sheep are bright red.

Next morning, after a comfortable stay, Mrs R watched in fascination my 'get ready to go' technique.

First - strap water bottle around hips and do up hip belt. Lean back and slip a bit of cut-up bedroll behind back to cushion the bony vertebrae (normal ones) and put another wad somewhere above right shoulder to cushion Egyptian vertebra. Slip pads on top of shoulders to cushion bones sticking up there. Push umbrella through belt. Hang fluorescent gauntlets on belt to become more visible to traffic. Do not put on woolly hat, although it is a cold wind, because a sheep is wearing my woolly hat.

I had to walk along the road again, but not for

long this time. I met a one-eyed man. He was quite young, but a bit strange. He offered me a cup of tea, but I politely declined, had a small and bizarre chat with him, then hurried on, before he could attach himself to me. People do that at times, especially when walking by myself – attach themselves to me. The odder they are, the more firmly they stick. Sometimes, I feel like a bit of flypaper. One of my friends once remarked that like attracts like, but I rejected that explanation out of hand.

After a few miles, I thankfully turned off the busy road onto a small one, veering inland to Bonar Bridge. It was a beautiful, isolated but never lonely road because, by myself like this, I'm never lonely. At first, I passed through grey trees, covered in lichen, with moss-covered rocks in between. Tendrils of lichen hung down. It was ogre country. I had only seen hanging lichen in such quantities before like that in the South Island, New Zealand. No wonder lots of Scots people had emigrated to that part of the world because it has many similarities to Scotland.

Later, I walked over completely barren, rounded hills, past Lock Buidhe. There were no trees, but two rows of pylons, marching along, to Inverness I suppose. When I passed under a row, I could hear a crackling and my hair stood up a bit.

Once, when I was young, I thought that all Japanese people looked the same but, when I visited there and after I'd got used to the set of their features, realised that they all look very different. Now, with so much opportunity to study them, I saw that it was the same with pylons. On first sight, they all look the same, but when you get used to them it can be seen that they all have different expressions. There they stand patiently. Some are smiling, some are sullen, some are casual, some are serious, but all of them are doing their best – doing their job. Like the Japanese.

I came upon a house, in the middle of nowhere. The view out of the back windows of the house would be of barren hills. From the front, the view was of two rows of pylons.

I stopped and ate a very nice pasty I had bought in Golspie. Some crumbs fell. Some little creature would feast on those and I wondered if it was possible that I had saved a whole species from extinction. It could be that there were very small microscopic creatures around me, fast dying out for lack of a suitable food supply and this sudden manna from heaven had saved them and given the help they needed to carry on and multiply.

Or, on the other hand, maybe a large crumb from the pasty had fallen on the head of one of the last of a mating pair and killed it, so I could have been responsible for the ending of a species.

How would I ever know? Everything I do sets in motion a chain leading to future events happening. Every action I take affects something else. I can't help that.

So far, I had been very lucky with the weather, because although cold with a bitter east wind, there had been no rain and it had even been sunny at times. With bad weather, it could have been hell over those isolated parts that I had been walking but instead, it had been marvellous. A colder temperature was much better for walking than if it was too hot. Now though, just before Bonar Bridge, I felt tired and it looked like rain was coming in and fast. There was a B & B sign up a road to my right. It was half a mile out of my way and uphill too, but I took the risk and it was worth it for the welcome I got from Lowe there. I wasn't expecting a meal, but Elenor said it was no trouble and soon, I was sitting down gratefully to good food.

I felt two emotions staying there on this working farm. One was contentment and cosiness, as I was in a good place and not sleeping outside in the cold and wet, for now it was raining hard. The other emotion was sadness, because of it being a farm and the young couple here reminded me of the young couple we used to be when first on our farm and how it could have been. A useless thing, this regret for the past and I hate it when it happens. Nothing can change it all now, it's gone and pointless to grieve over it because that will make the present time less happy. It doesn't happen so often now, this regret and sadness but, like when a person is getting used to living without a loved one around, just sometimes, something will suddenly trigger the memory.

I don't get so concerned about emotions these days though. Once, I used to and they took on more importance than they deserved, ruling my life. Now, I see them for what they are – transitory things, coming and going like clouds and its only when I give them importance that they solidify. In a day of walking, I can be happy, sad, angry, hopeful, desolate, confident, joyful – all over quite a short period and just floating through. It changes so quickly and I just go with it because it's not important.

So it was with this sad and regretful feeling, for it soon floated away.

I sank into a comfortable bed and slept well but, during the night, woke to a strange experience. I had pulled the curtains together and that made it pitch dark in the room.

Now, I like the dark. I hate sleeping with any light around. I miss the darkness where I live, because the darkness of the night is polluted by lights and now, security lights are on houses everywhere. I even go in search of the dark, standing in fields and woods, just to feel the enveloping warmth of it, so I was surprised that waking up here, with black all around, I suddenly felt fear.

Always in the dark though, I can see different shades of it, lighter in some places, deep black in others, but now, it was just – black! I felt that I couldn't breathe, like I was being crushed and thought that this is how it would be for someone trapped underground with the utter suffocating black blackness all around them. It would be a battle to subdue this fear and think clearly. It was like I had a memory of this feeling and it wasn't a good one. I wondered if blind people live in this total blackness, or do they register some lightness, so that it would be a lighter darkness?

I felt my way to the curtains and opened them a crack, so that I could see a different shade of darkness and then, it was fine and I went back to sleep.

Next morning, I set off happily enough, but soon found that I felt a bit 'down'. It wasn't serious, just one of the floating feelings. I saw that it was about 25 miles to a likely place for accommodation at Alness. I didn't reckon on doing that distance, about 15 miles was all I liked to do with that heavy rucksack.

There was low cloud and I walked on and on through thick mist. There would have been beautiful views I should have thought, but could not see anything mist, except for the moor and bog to either side. It was very attractive in its mysteriousness though.

The day was cold and windy, too wet to sit and rest anywhere, so I put my body on 'automatic' and just walked. The spare bone hurt but was bearable. The rest of me was OK.

Cars loomed up out of the mist, so I had to be very watchful and aware all the time. Miles and miles I walked, with no buildings or shelter anywhere. There could have been some welcome shelter where I could sit and rest for a while close by for all I knew, but the mist made anything further than a few feet away invisible.

There had only been one place marked on the map for ten miles along from my start and that was Aultnamain Inn. I'd looked at this when planning the walk at home, wondering why an Inn should be the only thing marked for miles, but now I knew. There was nothing else to fill in a large gap on the map. I thought that, as it was the only hostelry for miles, it must be an alive, bustling, populated place, this Inn. After all, there was certainly no competition.

A notice loomed up out of the mist, announcing that I had reached my target and was at the Inn. The notice stated what was on offer. There was coffee, snacks, bar meals, camping and caravan facilities, holiday cottages and a warm welcome extended to all. It sounded great. The thought of a comfortable sit down and some food had got me through the last bit of walking to the Inn.

And - there it was, looming up out of the mist! I quickened my pace eagerly, but as I got nearer, a horrible realisation began to dawn. There didn't seem to be much sign of life. No lights shone out into the mist, there were no cars parked there and the whole place looked deserted. There must have been people living there because when I walked around the building, a dog barked at me from inside and a cat peered through a window anxiously at me. It was just past mid-day on a Friday, so I should have thought it would be open.

My heart sank. I knocked on the door hopefully, but no, there was no-one at the Inn. Maybe it was too early in the season,

I sat on a doorstep, which was not very sheltered, but the best place I could find and sulked. The mist turned to rain so I sulked some more. I defiantly ate some oat-cakes and made myself a cup of coffee, ignoring the cold stare of the cat, but it was cold sitting there and not comfortable, so I was soon off again.

Now, it was raining all right, but not so very badly. Two cars stopped and offered me a lift. How tempting that was! But I was very noble and thanked them for their kindness, explaining what I was doing and that I mustn't cheat. They smiled, with the sort of gentleness and tolerance that is reserved for people who are behaving very strangely but seem harmless enough, and drove on inside their nice warm, snug and dry vehicles.

Approaching Alness, I came down out of the mist and saw that I was surrounded by beautiful countryside. Now, I could probably find a barn or outbuilding, but I was so close to Alness that I might as well go on. I had not thought that I would have been walking this far and never intended to but, here I was, intentional or not, at Alness.

Ahead of me was a sight that filled me with joy – a B & B sign. I knocked on the door.

A lady opened the door and listened to my query as to whether she had a room for me.

"Oh no," she said, "I only have double rooms, no single."

I wondered how many more people were going to arrive that evening to take the double rooms, but she had a very superior accent and demeanour, so perhaps it was the backpack and my wet and bedraggled person that she didn't want. She did direct me to another B & B further on though. Maybe it was an enemy of hers.

I got to the other B & B, sort of dragging my feet along. The last half-mile had felt like ten. The pleasant lady who opened the door and who didn't seem at all threatened by my appearance apologised for the fact that she only had a very small room right at the top of the house.

There was no apology necessary. I was delighted and indeed, it was marvellous! There was a bed, tea-making equipment, TV, rest and warmth. What more could I want? Before I settled down, I toddled down the road to buy some food at a supermarket and phone home to all the family, to let them know I was all right. All was well with them too.

My children worry about me. I can't think why. I'm supposed to worry about them and, sometimes it's true, because that's what mothers do.

"I've rung you several times," my son complains sometimes. "But you've not been in!"

"Been out playing with my friends," I reply, truthfully.

Still, it's probably better for them to worry about whether Mum is sleeping comfortably in a bed, or in a bog, than have a sad little voice answer on the end of a phone, lonely and bored.

After comforting my family as to my well-being, I went back to sit happily on my bed in the little cosy loft room, watching television and stuffing my face.

Morning brought rain. I'd planned to walk on little roads to Inverness, but it was about 30 miles that way and it really made no difference as to whether the route was more beautiful or not because the mist was so thick that I wouldn't see anything of the country anyway. Also, there was more of a threat from cars in a mist like that when on a little road, whereas the A9 into Inverness would be dead boring, but apparently had a wide verge all the way and I could see cars coming towards me easily. It was much shorter that way too. So, weather dictated my choice of boredom but perhaps more safety.

The rain was not heavy, just there. It came straight down, with no wind, so I could use my umbrella and keep reasonably dry. The umbrella was in bright colours, so traffic could see me more clearly.

About three miles along, I came across some tea rooms. I stopped and had a cup of tea, then a horde of young men arrived, on the way to play rugby in Wick.

That cheered me up and I enjoyed pushing through these handsome young hunks to the exit, exchanging jokes and laughter along the way.

Just before Cromarty Firth, there was a visitor centre. This was getting to be a much better day than I had expected! Being forever an opportunist as far as a cup of tea is concerned, I stopped again and had a large piece of cake as well. It was very peaceful and pleasant there, with gentle environmentally friendly type music, which doesn't demand listening to but just colours the emotions to a shade of restfulness. I was the only one there. I supposed it wasn't a going-out to the countryside sort of day.

The music changed to Scots folk. When that was written and sung, it would have been a really hard, cold, wet life up here in the Highlands. The people singing that music around peat fires in their crofts could never have imagined the music being played in this comfortable, warm and amazing building, eating food that must surely, in those days, only have been experienced by royalty. And me a Sassenach too!

That was the end of the goodies. Now, it was just boring. I enlivened it by walking on the road until a car coming towards me reached a certain distance, then jumped up on the verge. I gave them plenty of time, so that they didn't have to swerve at all. It was a bit tiring, having to keep jumping up and down, but less than walking on the verge all the time, because that was often very uneven, so I had to be careful not to twist an ankle.

The cars got more numerous as the day went on, which was a bit stressful but within their rights, I suppose. I thought there would be bound to be bus stops along a main road like this, perhaps with shelters, so that I could stop and rest from time to time, but there were none. The best I could find was the occasional lay-by with a waste bin that I could turn my back on and alleviate the weight of my rucksack on it, while having a standing rest.

That cheap old umbrella earned its keep all day.

Once, with all that tea drinking, I had to do a pee, but there was nowhere secluded. I could see a little road ahead, which branched off on my side and a telephone box just round the corner. When I reached it, I hid as best I could around the back of the telephone box, but cars kept coming round the corner, so had to keep standing up, trying to look like a lamp-post. Then a gust of wind whooshed at me, right at the wrong time, and I got my knickers all wet. Men are definitely technically at an advantage at times like this.

By the time I got to Tore, which was about sixish miles short of Inverness, I'd had enough, so stopped at the Kilroy Arms there. It was just within my budget, but worth it because it was so beautiful. Jo there gave my wet person a warm welcome and put my clothes in the washing machine, which was marvellous, then gave me tea and we sat chatting.

Usually, when I get to a B & B, I have a system. I shower, or bath myself first. Then, I wash out a T-shirt, knickers, socks maybe, silk shirt occasionally, giving them as much time as possible to dry. If there is wallpaper, I'm very careful not to hang the wet clothes where the damp from their drying would cause it to absorb the damp and come off. I treat other peoples homes in the manner in which I should like them to treat mine, which sounds very holier than thou and smug, but really, I think should be standard behaviour. Respect for other human beings must improve the world and that can't be a bad thing.

After the cleanliness bit, I see to food and rest and check out where I'll be walking the next day, write my diary, watch TV if there is one and generally relax.

I did well to stop here at Tore, because my body was beginning to show some danger signs but, with the rest and luxurious surroundings, was soon OK again.

Moreton, the landlord, knew the way I planned to take through the Grampians. I was very pleased, because I'd been a bit worried about that. It looked like it could be wild and isolated and I only had the trainers as footwear and a very vague map for the footpath bit. Now, though, looking at his maps and talking about it, I felt happy enough. That precious compass around my neck is my biggest saviour.

Moreton was a mine of interesting information and I learned many things.

People came up here after the ice age from the Mediterranean. It can be seen from the terrain how sparse and separated the people must have been. Hard, hard, hard, compared to our cushy life now. I suppose the separateness of the groups led to the different clans. It was some Irish, who came over and were called Scots, who gave rise to the name Scotland to be given to the land. The Picts, who were there before, had no writing so, despite rumours, had not invented the ballpoint pen.

Highland cattle mature for meat slowly, so the farmers here were hit hard by the BSE rulings for early slaughter. As if it wasn't hard enough farming here anyway. Moreton also tells of how untreated milk has been and still is, infected with TB sometimes here. When he was young, he said, two thirds of the pupils in a class would die from it. Indeed, his own children contracted TB from milk, but by then, it was easily cured, and so they were. Now, he said, the disease is back, but resistant to antibiotics and killing again.

Bacteria are bad enough, but viruses now. They are really clever little devils. Sort of animal and sort of mineral, marvellous mimics, they can stay dormant for vast stretches of time, in the most inhospitable conditions. Like outer space, for instance. They could lurk inside dust clouds with no trouble at all and, when the earth passes through a cloud (as it sometimes does), well now, there's a whole new way of life opening up for an ambitious virus.

Comet tails too. They could be full of the things. Fred Hoyle put forth the theory, many years ago, that some epidemics in the past, seemingly springing up at the same time in different areas of the world, without the benefit of modern transport, could be due to viruses coming in from outer space. On the positive side, some think that life itself could have been seeded on the earth from space.

So, there you are. That's something else you can think and worry about.. When the worries of your own life have eased off a bit and you've worried yourself into an impasse about greenhouse heating / ozone depletion / being zapped by a meteor / comet/nuclear weapons / nearby supernova explosion / sun flares / falling space debris / someone falling from a top storey / running out of coffee – why, then you can have a really good worry about viruses coming in from outer space and wiping out the lot of us. It's always a worry to have nothing to worry about, so wise to have a really good one to fall back on.

* * *

Today was to be a Big Achievement Day. I was reaching Inverness, which was not so far really, but a milestone, because it was back to where I came in by plane.

It didn't seem as far as six and a half miles on the pleasant, small road I took from Tore. There was no rain either. The sun came out and it became quite hot. Altogether, it was a very good walk until I came to Inverness, where the way I took turned out to be industrial and busy. I kept my eyes peeled for large spiders.

It was Sunday, but there were quite a few shops open in the shopping precinct, so I hung around there for a while, phoning people and writing cards. I was keeping my friend Joyce up to date with my route, because all my friends in Ashdown Ramblers were very interested and concerned for my welfare. I had been quite taken aback by the warm concern felt from them all. I had not expected anybody to be interested much in the walk because it was my own self indulgence, but their warmth and well-wishes were with me all the time.

Apparently, they were amazed at my quick progress and very impressed by it. So was I. What they didn't realise though, was that the progress was not because of ability or intention, but because of the sinking into bog problem and that it had been too cold or wet to sit down for long and rest on the way. This had caused me to cover much more territory than I perhaps otherwise would have done.

Inverness is the capital of the Highlands. Dating right back to 1180, King William of Lyon granted a charter to King Brude. Saint Columba came visiting, but King

Brude wouldn't open the gates, so Saint C. made the sign of the cross and the gate flew open. King Brude was impressed and became converted. So would I be impressed, but I'd want to learn how to do that for if I locked the car keys inside the car or the door key inside the house.

Saint C. also subdued the Loch Ness Monster. This creature had already killed a man and had a go at Saint C., who again made the sign of the cross and the terrified monster fled. Something to do with kilts, I suspect. Even the Picts were impressed. "Come again," they said. There was no mention of Saint Columba subduing large spiders.

I felt full of energy after my rest and learning all those interesting things, so continued on through Inverness. The spare bone was behaving itself, probably sulking, but now I didn't have the pain of that to worry about, my shoulders felt sore. It's funny how pain from one part of the body can be ignored if there is more pain in another part. Once, I had a bad headache and sat in some stinging nettles. There was no particular reason for sitting in the nettles, it was an accident, but I didn't notice the headache too much after that. My attention had shifted downwards, so perhaps that's what I should do when the bone hurts or my shoulders feel sore – sit in some nettles.

I looked for General Wades Military Road, but couldn't see any sign of it, so asked a passing lady.

"No," she said. She'd lived here for 20 years and couldn't remember ever seeing it. I walked on a short way and, there it was, a sign with an arrow stating clearly "Footpath to Military Road." The lady had walked right by it and had probably been doing so for 20 years without seeing it. Now isn't that amazing? Or, maybe she couldn't read. People don't like to admit that.

I often ask directions, but never just ask one person if there are more around. Sometimes, people will confidently send me in the opposite direction. I've suffered too many times from that, so ask about three people if I can and take the average answer. Recommended short cuts are often lethal, so I usually smile politely, thank the person and ignore the advice about the short cut completely.

You see, they know the area well. "Take the left turning," they say, quite forgetting that there are two other left turns before the one they meant, one of which leads to the sewage works and the other in a long circle to somewhere before where you are now. It's like one of those board games. 'Go to sewage works. Drop back a space.'

Anyway, safe on the Military Road now, I headed towards Daviot. It started raining. The track stopped and continued as a footpath which was pleasant, but was overhung with wet bushes and trees, all keen on fondly caressing me, so the umbrella was very useful in diverting the drips.

I plodded on and on, starting to think about stopping, but there was no promising looking shelter anywhere. Then, I met a man with a dog, who said that Daviot was only a mile away, so that seemed good.

Two miles later, I realised that the man had been talking in Scots miles. That was something else I had discovered. Half an English Mile = One Scots Mile (if you're lucky and the person isn't trying to encourage you by making it shorter). People up here most definitely used the Scots mile.

Another thing that seems to happen often is being told "Oh, it's just up the road, not far," but one hour and tired legs later, you realise they're talking about how long it takes in a car, not walking.

However, Scots miles not withstanding, I finally reached Daviot, where somebody directed me to a B & B. The lady who opened the door was sorry, but she was fully booked. It was raining heavily by now and I must have looked so dejected that she phoned another nearby. Where I was then was on a small road running parallel to the main road. The other B & B was only opposite, over the main road, but either a walk across a very wet field with no way through, or quite a longish walk in a hairpin curve, so she insisted on driving me around to it, which I thought was very kind. I had just enough food for the evening and hoped to stock up the next day.

I had found that it was difficult getting the food right. Sometimes I carried the extra weight of food all day and discovered that I could have got some where I stopped for the night, or sometimes, I thought there would be a shop for certain where I was heading, but there wasn't. So many village shops have shut down now.

Next day, I walked the longer way, down an old road, which was very peaceful. It was marvellous countryside around and the temperature was perfect for walking.

I passed by a large stone, in which was embedded a shaft of iron and puzzled as to how the iron had got in there. Perhaps it was a modern Excalibur, so I had a go at pulling it out, but it didn't budge. Obviously, I was not the chosen one.

Then, I passed a small lake, where I felt a 'presence'. That's all I can say about it really. I can't explain exactly what I felt more than that. There was something though and it was strange, but not frightening. The woods I passed had this atmosphere too. There was a lot of moss and lichen and I went into the woods a bit, which was not far because they were the tussocks and bog sort and I sat a while, not minding a wet bum, because I liked this feeling (the atmosphere, that is, not the wet bum).

Sometimes, when I am on a walk, I get an 'atmosphere' of a place. Mostly, there doesn't seem to be any reason. It's usually when I'm just thinking mundane thoughts or not thinking much of anything. Nor is it usually anywhere where there seems to be anything special, like rocks or standing stones. It happens that I will simply be walking through woods or, perhaps, not woods and, suddenly, it's like stepping over a sharply defined boundary – it will feel totally different. Occasionally, it's not a good feeling, as though something doesn't want me there and then I move on quickly but mostly, it's a good feeling and I stop for a time. Then, when I move on, I will soon take a step and will be out of the area, just like that. I've tried walking back 'in' and I can. It's like a different coloured patch, except the 'colour' is an atmosphere.

After this quiet and atmospheric walk, I had to go along the main road for a bit and did not enjoy that at all. It was almost like a shock to the system, after the mysterious woods, all that metal rushing by, in a hurry to get somewhere, then in a hurry to get back again.

When I thought of my life at home, I remembered how often I seemed to be in a rush and I didn't like that. Having time to think about it now, I analysed why it was that I found myself in that hurry. Some of it seemed to be my own doing, trying to do too much and leaving myself too little time. Why? What did I gain by that? I certainly didn't enjoy things more by having to rush around, so what a waste of time.

The other cause of hurry appeared to be the 'quick, quick, quick,' imposed on me by other people's needs and their own haste. I decided to try and stop both of these when I got back, because, walking along now, without any complications, it seemed to be such stupid behaviour.

Luckily, it wasn't very far to walk on the main road, because I had an 'I hate cars' day. When I'm in that mood, I find it really unreasonable that any cars should be on the road when I wanted to walk along it. I hate it when they string themselves out, making me walk on the bumpy verge all the time. It's much better when they come along in a bunch, leaving a nice long gap before the next bunch, so I can walk on the even road surface. If they were considerate, they'd do that all the time.

I was having a grumpy phase. The wind was against me, making it harder to walk, but I came off the big road at Tomatin and looming up in front of me, like a mirage in a desert, was a Little Chef. Indulgence in the type of food that is bad for a person and lots of tea soon dissipated the grumps.

I reached Carrbridge and decided that I liked it very much. There were lots of places to stay. I was spoilt for choice but chose one that was just an ordinary smallish house, because it looked just like an ordinary smallish house. It fulfilled its looks together with the lovely, homely couple there that I felt very much at ease with.

Next day, there were silver rocks all around me. They glinted in the sun, wet with the showers, like fairyland. It was muscovite mica that was making them look silver. Daffodils and primroses were everywhere, in their flush. They had been finished at home when I left, now I was getting a second helping, which suited me. Violets had been everywhere too, all along the way, but bluebells were just beginning, in sheltered places. People had been telling me that it was much colder than usual for May, but it was good for walking.

I walked past Slochd, which, as well as having a very odd name, was high and exposed. Apparently, one winter, lots of people had been stranded there, stuck in the snow. I could well imagine it. Again, I thought of what a terribly hard life it must have been in the 'good old days', just trying not to starve, or get killed by other people. In winter, if you hadn't already died of starvation, being killed by other people, or pneumonia, you'd have probably died of boredom. Captain Burt, bless his heart, wrote in the 1730's about the life led by the Gaelic speaking people here. He said,

…..”Are in winter often confined to their Glens by swollen Rivers, Snow or Ice, have no Diversions to amuse them, but sit brooding in the Smoke over the Fire till their Legs and Thighs are scorched to an extraordinary Degree, and many have Sore Eyes and some are quite Blind.”

I suppose it could have been worse. They could have been forced to watch Australian sitcoms all winter.

Again, I was walking alongside mysterious woods. It was raining on and off, but as long as sometimes it was off, that was OK. How I love these woods. Again, I tried to walk into them, but didn't get very far. I needed wellies to explore more. It looked very green in there. Even the light looked green and I loved the earthy smell and the sound of drips all around. It would be good to be unencumbered by this heavy body that feels the cold and wet, pain and discomfort. Without that body, I could float around in these woods, in the green light filtering through the trees.

I've often thought how wonderful to be able to move, bodiless like that, amongst ice cliffs and chasms of beautiful frozen wastes without being cold. And then, after sampling all the jungles, deserts and icy regions on earth and exploring the depths of the oceans, I could drift among the galaxies and see what's out there.

But now, I had to content myself with walking

towards Aviemore. The Grampians ahead still had quite a lot of snow on them. They looked a bit bleak and scary. Soon, I would be crossing them, with my heavy old body in tow.

I had intended to stop at Aviemore and have the afternoon off, but when I got there, it was half shut. It seemed it was too late for skiers and too early for summer tourists. Anyway, I didn't feel attracted to stay, so had some fish and chips and moved on.

There was a small loch just before Alvie and a memorial to three young men, all 27 years old, who drowned there in 1980. I wondered why all three had drowned, because it was only a small loch and easy enough to swim to the edge, I should have thought. All of them drowning seemed strange.

I got to Kincraig and the Suie Hotel. Wendy there didn't know why the young men had drowned but told me the way to the village of Kincraig proper and Loch Insh. She said it was well worth going so, even though I was tired, I made the effort and she was quite right, it was worth it. The village was delightful, just as villages should be, with the church high up on a hill. The church dated back to the 7th century and was the site of an ancient place of worship, before it became a church. It overlooked the Loch and was very peaceful. I stayed for a while in the evening sun, with the hills and woods all around and the rippling water of the Loch glistening like gold. Silver rocks and gold water. A rich country indeed.

There was a wooded island in the Loch and Wendy had told me to look for an osprey nest there. I could see it, a collection of twigs high up in a tree. It was very large and very untidy looking. I waited for a time, but didn't see an osprey. I was very grateful to Wendy for encouraging me to come there, because it had been a beautiful experience. Kincraig is indeed a gem, which would be only too easy to pass by on the main road and even the quieter road I had walked along.

There were lots of books back at my lodgings, so I borrowed one to read about the Osprey.

Apparently, it has special spines on the soles of its feet to help grip slippery fish. The birds winter over in West Africa and come back here in March/April and often use the same nest year after year, adding to it, which accounts for its large size. The eggs are white, boldly blotched with deep chocolate and are so pretty that egg collectors and trophy hunters almost brought the poor bird to extinction, but in 1955, a pair returned to nest at Loch Garten and now their numbers are increasing again. To catch food, it circles, dives and submerges (they have been known to drown when their claws have stuck). Then, it resurfaces (if it hasn't drowned), shakes its plumage violently and flies off, but I didn't see that. They can live to 32 years old

I slept well, probably dreaming that I was an osprey, but couldn't remember..

* * *

Today was going to be an easy one to Kingussie. It was only six miles and, there I would stop. It was good weather until I got there, but then started raining heavily.

On the way, I had felt a bit homesick. That was OK. It was in order and, in a strange way, felt as though that was how it should be. It made me think how simple my life was now in many ways. As I walked along, there was no sticky stuff inside my head and my mind was clear. Any thoughts of past and future just drifted through without sticking and it felt sort of clean inside there.

I thought about people and problems, including myself. There had been times when I had been through a bad patch, like most people encounter at some time in their lives. I had got together with others in a group and we shared our problems, talking them out and helping each other.

That had been valuable and I started to heal, but then it went a bit too far and stopped being helpful. In fact, it became harmful. It did not seem to be happily accepted that I was feeling much more clear and happy but that I must still have the problems deep inside, covered up but still unresolved. Anything I said was not heard as simply what I meant, but was analysed and dissected. This confused me because I usually know exactly what I am saying and why. If I don't, I say so.

After a while, I stopped going to these gatherings, because it was almost as if the 'stuck' people wanted me to stay inside my problems too.

Once, I'd said to a 'leader' happily that I had no

problems at the moment, only difficulties.

"Huh!" she had replied sharply. "Then perhaps you had better look more deeply into yourself."

Again, there was an occasion when someone had looked at me fiercely for a while and announced, "I think you have a lot of anger inside."

"No," I had replied, "I don't", because it had changed. True that I still got angry at times, but it was very different, not very important and was only temporary.

"You're just covering it up," she had said, ignoring my words. "I can see its there."

"No, it's not."

"It's there. I know. I can tell."

"No! I'm not angry!"

"There you are,' my accuser had said triumphantly. "I told you it was there."

There were all these 'experts' claiming to know better about what I felt than I did myself, based usually on how they had decided I should be feeling and then giving me advice I hadn't asked for. It was a sort of violence, this advice, smashing at me whether I wanted it or not and it had made me very depressed for a time.

Then, I realised, it was just like sub-nuclear particles really. People put a lot of energy into looking for one of these particles, then the energy they put in is converted into mass and bingo – there's a particle. They've created it by looking for it.

So it was the same with problems, if you weren't careful. Look too hard for them and there they are, just waiting for the energy to be put into the searching to make them solid if they are small and tenuous, or even create them if they are not there.

It could happen that I would go into these gatherings with not much wrong, but come out tearful and with problems that I hadn't had before I'd walked in!

It doesn't happen now though, because I solved that. I don't go. I've got confidence that the best person to say how I'm feeling, is me. Life throws up difficulties to me like it does to everyone else, but I try to keep them to their proper size. They like to be fed, but if you refuse to feed them, they usually slink away, sulking. That sounds very smug – sometimes I fail but I know the theory!

Kingussie was a good place to be. It was early closing day, but there were still places open. I found a Bunkhouse Hostel, which was excellent – clean, bright and cheap. I was the only person in a four-bedroom dormitory, so that was good too.

I deposited my heavy weight and tripped lightly, without a care, to the folk museum, just up the road. That was brilliant. There was a re-created 'black house', with a peat fire inside, just like there would have been in the past. I went inside, but soon came out choking and with eyes streaming, suffering from what felt like the equivalent of five years passive smoking.

The traditionally dressed lady outside laughed as I came out so rapidly and told me that the people then only lived to about 35. I was not surprised. Chairs were very low she said, so that they could hopefully sit below the smoke line. As far as I could see, even ants would not be below the smoke line.

I went then, into the farm museum, which was like a long barn. An attendant came scuttling out, because she saw from a camera screen when somebody came in. She smiled at me, walked to the other side of a screen and came back, looking puzzled.

"There was somebody else with you," she said.

She said she was certain she had seen somebody on the screen.

I assured her that I was on my own, but it could be she saw someone all the same.

She edged away and left me with a space between us, but I knew what I meant. Whether its imagination or whether its not, the fact is, I always feel that I have a companion when I'm alone and I don't mean that in a weird or ghost-like way. I don't really know what I mean really, only that it feels like another person is there, completely non-obtrusive and so like being alone too. I don't mind them being there, in fact, I welcome it, because I feel that I'm being looked after in some way. Various people who have been sane and ordinary and not given to undue imagination, have glimpsed this companion and told me, but I have never seen anything myself, just felt it.

I don't really care whether this is real or not because the effect is good. When I had started to get anxious about where I was going to stay for the night, I had felt effect and knew it will be all right and it always had been so far. It might not be comfortable, where I end up, but it's all right. I've learned to think positively that there will be a place for me to stay, one way or another and that I will be safe. Its there, that place, waiting for me to arrive. So far, anyway, all has been well.

I felt very happy in Kingussie. The next day was to be the hard bit through the Grampians. I had felt apprehensive about that and usually, when I feel apprehension, it proves to be for a good reason, but there was a large scale map of the area at the Hostel, so I could have a good look at where I'd be going and that reassured me a bit.

I bought food in readiness for three days, but had been assured that the water was pure enough to drink up there.

It was a good start in the morning, with nice weather. A bit of wasted energy was put out when I tried to cut off a corner by a footpath which disappeared at a ravine, so I had to go back again and around by the original and longer route.

I joined the old drover's road which led towards snow capped mountains. There was wild land all around, with a rushing river to my right.

Happily walking in supposed isolation, I gave a loud and satisfying burp as walkers are apt to do when alone and not caring. This was the cue for a young man, unheard by me and grinning broadly, to stride up from behind. Oh well, it could have been worse.

He was doing a circular walk, but on the same track for a while, so we walked together and sat to eat in companionship. He gave me some very nice local cake.

He told me he was a prison officer, but that he was intending to retire as soon as he reached the permitted age. This was because there were such a high number of prison officers who died very young, in their fifties, through stress induced heart attacks. He didn't want to do that. He wanted to enjoy his life and family for many years. I appreciated his company and waved as he struck out up the hill to the left. He was wearing green and muted colours and I was amazed at how quickly he merged into the background, so that soon, I couldn't see where he was at all.

After that, I walked towards the mountains, which were very close now. It was black, black, black in front of me – a sharp division of weather from fine to not good at all and I soon walked into seriously wet conditions. The rain was heavy, but at least it was straight down and the umbrella helped.

I was heading towards Glaick Lodge. This whole area did not have a good write-up. You could say, it had a reputation to live up to.

Glaick is one of the highest lodges in Scotland. Apparently, through the ages, all around there has been the haunt of the occult and supernatural. There is a Witch of

Gaick and one night, a hunter, staying in a hut there and who had two hounds with him, heard a scratching at the door. When he opened it, there was a bedraggled cat standing there. His hounds would have set about it and quite right too, but the cat spoke, saying it was the repented witch. It scared him silly and only goes to show that you shouldn't open the door to strange cats.

The Leannan Sith (Fairy Sweetheart) would come to hunters and she could harm the wife of anyone who fell in love with her. Nasty.

In 1799, Captain John MacPherson of Ballachroan, with four attendants and deer hounds, stayed at a bothy in Gaick one Christmas. They did not return. The bothy was torn to pieces and there were large stones that had fallen within a couple of hundred yards around. The bodies were later found and it looked as though the onslaught had been very sudden, although there had been no apparent threat to the building from rock falls or anything else and it had been in a sheltered position. Before the disaster, the unfortunates had seen a fire on the hillside that wasn't there. (I reckon myself it was a shower of meteorites but that is a more comforting theory.)

So perhaps it wasn't surprising that I had a feeling of apprehension, with that sort of history. Local people hesitated to go there and now, there I was, defying rain and witches and approaching Gaick Lodge.

I hadn't known what to expect and somehow had hoped that perhaps I could have stayed at Gaick in an outhouse or something. There was a young man there, in charge of the place. He seemed very young to me, which only proved that I was getting old! He was obviously a bit worried about me staying around, because of his responsibility there, but assured me that there would be a place to stay at a bit further on. The next lodge was derelict now, he said, but there was a bothy further on where people could stay. He had stayed in it himself, only the previous weekend.

This bothy was only about three miles further, he said. I could see, by looking at my map, that he was talking Scots miles because it looked like five but didn't have a lot of choice in the matter so, after a short rest, set off again. The young man told me that it had been raining solidly for days up there.

I came to a stream that should have been easy to cross, but it had so much water now that I was going to have to get my feet wet, except the young man and a friend came along in a land-rover, off to do some fishing and gave me a lift across.

Later, I walked past the loch, where they were sitting in a boat, in the rain, patiently fishing. This was Loch Vrodin I believed and another legend attached to that.

A hunter had become the owner of a litter of fairy pups but, before they were grown up a demon took all but one. The demon handicapped the remaining pup by breaking a leg – poor little puppy, nasty demon. The name of the pup was Brodan. Now, a white fairy deer lived on Ben Alder and this the hunter hunted, because if there is something beautiful, you can be sure a hunter wants to hunt and kill it. They found the deer. There was a long chase and the dog and deer reached Lock Vrodin together and both plunged in. The hound caught up the elfin deer and seized it. Both disappeared under the water. The lake was named after the hound, although it didn't look the same name to me, only similar. Nobody enquired after the name of the deer.

A strange little story that, the meaning of which (if there be any), completely escapes me. Anyway, I didn't see either hound or deer, only the two young men fishing in the rain. Well – I think they were two young men .....

I carried on, pleased that I had kept my feet dry, but this joy was a bit premature because, shortly afterwards, there was another stream, streaming and, this time, I did get them wet. It was obvious that the constant rain had caused the rivers to rise and they were still rising. It was a bit worrying. I gave up trying to cross by stones and keep my feet dry, it was safer to accept that I was going to get a lot wetter still and wade. A rucksack can be dangerous because, if you fall in the water, it could drag you down, so it's best to hang it on one shoulder so that, in the worst case, you'd be able to get shot of it.

Then, the track came to an end and somewhere up ahead was the footpath that I must take. I couldn't see where the footpath was, because it was just peat-like stuff all around and very wet. I knew that I would have to cross the river though, because the footpath was on the other side and down the side of the loch the river flowed into.

I floundered along the edge of the river, looking for the safest way to cross and chose a place where the flow looked slightly less turbulent.

It was not a happy experience because the river was rushing along pretty violently, but the trusty umbrella served as a balancing stick and I made it, but only just, with water above my knees. The current had been very strong though and now, I had to hope that there wasn't any worse up ahead, because I knew I wouldn't be able to cross with safety. Looking around, there was not anywhere inviting to stay the night either, it was all very exposed to wind and rain, very very wet and soggy.

I found the footpath easily enough, except that 'small stream' would have been a better description.

I was very tired indeed by now and the way seemed never ending, but finally I saw the buildings of the old lodge ahead and there, at the start of them, was the bothy. I was extremely happy to see it.

You wouldn't believe though, that some so-and-so had put a high fence all along for quite a way, so that I couldn't walk straight to the bothy. Oh no! I had to drag my weary limbs all the way along the fence, through a gate that was hard to open and all the way back along inside the length of the fence again. I began to feel as if I was on some sort of commando test.

The bothy had a fireplace and a small wood store. There was another, larger store outside, with logs in it and there was a saw, but the blade was broken, so I gathered as much of the small bits of branches and scrapings as I could and soon had a fire going. I should have got some more to replenish the store, but it was all so very wet around and my footwear was not suitable for such activity, so I gave myself up to selfish pleasure.

The fire was cheerful and therapeutic. There was a comfortable couch to sleep on and a chair. The water from the river was brown, but certainly there was plenty of it and it added colour and flavour to the nice warming soup I made.

The mountains were all around, rearing up and clear to see for a while, but then, the cloud got lower and lower, until everything was obscured by the cloud and rain. I felt very safe and cosy in my bothy, grateful to be there and didn't even think of witches disguised as cats or large stones raining down.

I was a bit reluctant to leave that snug little bothy the next morning, because I liked it there. I was even more reluctant to put on the still wet socks and shoes, but knew it was pointless to waste dry ones, because they'd soon be wet again. Ugh! There's not much more uncomfortable than putting on cold and wet socks and trainers.

I'd found that my water bottle had sprouted a leak, so drank a lot before I started and carried it empty.

The weather was much better, but I was right about the feet, because I soon had to cross another stream. It was not so very deep this time though and the water only just seeped into my shoes.

I walked towards light skies. Looking back at the high mountains, clouds were covering the tops and it looked very black in that direction. It was a bit like walking through the thickness of a sandwich, light white bread each side and marmite in the middle. Now though, it was very pleasant, with amazing views, reminding me of a low bit of the Himalayas.

After a while, I thought it safe to change into dry socks and my spare trainers. Boy, that felt good. As I sat changing them, I heard a whoosh, whoosh, whoosh, and looked up to see a majestic and graceful arc of geese passing overhead.

It was a good day, on small, small roads and beautiful, with trees covering the slopes and little giggling streams. I got very thirsty and was about to head for one of the streams, but came upon a house and the lady there kindly filled my water bottle. I drank and drank, before it all leaked out again.

It was a very steep, winding road to Trinafour. When I got there, I saw how it had got its name. There are so few houses there, you say to yourself, "Why, there's only tri," then you see another – "Na, there's four." Hence, Tri-na-four. There were really a few more houses than that, but not many.

Never believe road signs. The people who put the mileage on them are living in a little Universe of their own. I had seen one that had stated proudly, Trinafour 4m. A mile further on, it said Trinafour 5m. Was I walking backwards? Had time reversed?

I was on a beautiful road now to Tummel Bridge, with grand views of the Grampians, streaked with snow. Silver birch were wearing their new clothes, standing out in brilliant emerald green against the background of grey and white striped mountains.

The road was an easy downhill for three whole miles. I tried not to think that what goes down will probably go up again the other side and just enjoyed the easy walking.

At Tummel Bridge, there was a caravan and camping site. I asked if there was a place to stay there and they said there wasn't, but that only a few yards away, there was a B & B and the kind people at the office kindly phoned there to see if there was a place for me. Which there was.

Margaret greeted me so kindly, with tea, cake and biscuits. She put my wet trainers out to dry and generally spoiled me.

Really good times had come. After a good old washing of all of me, I went to the camping site launderette, which they had said I could use. There, I stripped down to one T-shirt and shorts and put everything washable, including my fleece and coat, into the machine. I sat and read a book, shivering. Then came the tumble dryer. That was better, because I could lean against the warmth of it. It was just like that advert on TV, where the man takes off all his clothes and sits waiting for the washing to be done, except that it was too cold to take off all my clothes.

I knew that the silk shirts and trousers would dry quickly, so hooked them out of the tumble dryer as soon as I could and put them on, feeling the blissful warmth. It was not very long before all the rest were dry too and soon, me and all my clothes, smelled fresh and sweet. What happiness! It was a great feeling, magnified by the tough time I'd had the day before.

It goes like that. For a while it can be hard and perhaps miserable, but in not too long, it can change to comfortable and happy. And of course, the other way around. Now, adding even more to my well being, I got a take-away at the campsite shop. Margaret gave me a pot of coffee to go with it. I liked Tummel Bridge very much.

I set off the next day, glowing from kind treatment and in dry shoes, smelling like a fresh field after rain, and thinking about walking a few 'short' days.

I had phoned all the family to let them know I was safe because I'd told them the route I was taking through the mountains and said that, if they didn't hear from me within a few days, to start searching. You have to be sensible if you know you'll be in an isolated area by yourself. When I'm on little roads, there is no problem, because somebody would surely notice my exhausted and emaciated body crawling along on all fours. If the kind people I had met so far were anything to go by, they would find the time to tend to a collapsed walker.

That morning, I thought I was starting a migraine. I get these at regular intervals and usually they last two days, but I just go through them, because now that I'm almost grown up, they are much better than they used to be and I can function. This time, it cleared very quickly, only lasting half a day, which was marvellous.

Migraines and headaches are different. I get headaches a lot, usually waking up with one that mostly clears, but sometimes doesn't. On this walk though, I had not had one headache so far. It always happens when I'm walking that, despite ill treating my body with a heavy rucksack and walking long distances, often living on junk food, I'm very clear in my head and healthy and don't get the headaches. That must be telling me something.

Another strange thing, peculiar to the walk, is that I'd been sleeping very well (except when out in the cold) and hadn't remembered any dreams. That is very unusual because I don't sleep very well at home, but often have several dreams in one night, which I can usually remember if I want to. I expect that sleeping lightly, the dreams are more easily remembered.

I had been kindly sent off today with a banana and plastic bottle to replace the leaking water bottle.

Soon, I paid for the three miles downhill the day before. Newton's 6th law manifested itself. That is, the Law of Anti-Gravity. 'What goes down must go up again.'

Most people think there are only three Newtonian Laws. This of course is not true. After Newton's death, a secret hidden manuscript was found by his brother, Crawley Newton, giving Laws 4, 5 and 6. No.4 is 'Rubbish Expands to fill the Space Available' and No.5 is 'The intensity of the rain is in direct proportion to the distance you have left your raincoat.'

So, for the next three miles, I trudged upwards, but it was the start of the day and I was fresh and clean. I walked by gushing streams and woods and, as I got higher, looked over breathtaking views. Daffodils, narcissi and primroses were everywhere, together with the misty blue of emerging bluebells. In the distance were more hills. They must have been high, because they still had snow on them, but more rounded and undulating than the ones I had come through.

It was a day I could sit and rest comfortably. I came across a chair and table, hewn out of large logs and set back from the road. The chair was like a throne. I sat in it for a while, on high enough ground so that I was looking down at trees. There was the rushing of water below and I became aware of a humming sound. At first, I thought it was in my head, but concentrated on clearing the head noises and it was still there and all around me. I think it was some sort of harmonic from the rushing water. The sound made me feel very relaxed and sleepy.

As I sat, I was somewhere 'else' but also still there. It was a really good feeling.

After a while, I thought about how it would be if I was on a real, royal throne. A lot of people in the past have wanted to sit on a throne – have wanted power. Why do people want power? Power over other people? So many do. I like to be in control over my own life and hate it when I'm bounced about by other people, but I certainly don't want control over anybody else. Why should I, and why does anybody want this? It happens so much and I don't understand it. Sometimes I feel very bewildered by what people do to each other.

I walked on, feeling energetic after sitting in that place and all around me was the most beautiful land, with farms on hills and woods.

I reached Kenmore comfortably. It was a beautiful village, with a castle. The castle was now surrounded by a golf course, which felt a bit strange. It seemed to be a very popular village, but I soon found accommodation at the Old Police House and was comfortable yet again.

* * *

Gorse of course, lots of it. Apparently, it used to be used for feeding animals in the past, so I suppose that was why Scots people took it to New Zealand and created one big problem for the countryside there.

I was a bit short on green vegetables in my food supply and refused to eat gorse, but there was a constant supply of side salad along my way, bursting with minerals and vitamins. This was the humble stinging nettle, brought over by the Romans as a herb and taking to the British countryside with great gusto.

I eat stinging nettles as I go along. This is not crazy or painful. If you pick the more tender tops or upper leaves off very firmly, they don't sting at all. This is where the saying 'Grasping the nettle' came from. You have to be bold and not chicken-out half way or you will get stung.

Then, you roll the leaves very firmly, so that all the barbs are squashed. After that, you eat them. No problems. I only eat a few at a time, but am sure it helps my body.

There were slugs all over the road. Crossing from right to left. Crossing from left to right. I felt sorry for the poor little devils out on the tarmac, with the likelihood of being squashed by a passing car, or pair of trainers. I was tempted to put some of them back on the grass, but there were far too many, it would be a full time job. Also, how did I know it was not part of a slug way of life. This might be a rite of passage, an ordeal that has to be performed when reaching slughood. If I stopped them, I could be interfering and ruining some ancient slug tradition. Humans do that a lot, interfere, so I left the slugs in peace to do their own thing.

I was heading towards Amulree. It was a very steep climb at first then, suddenly, I was above the clouds. I cannot describe how very beautiful it was, with a mixture of rough, bare land and trees. I sat amongst trees, by a rushing stream, surrounded by a wild mixture of mounds and rocks.

A lamb had become separated from its mother, who was the other side of a stream. It ran up and down, looking for a place to cross and complaining bitterly. If I had tried to help it, I would have frightened it to a greater distance, but I had faith that it could help itself best and, sure enough, it found a way over and joined its mother who, I must say, hadn't seemed as concerned as she should have been.

When I got even higher, there was just – moor. In fact, there was nothing but moor for miles, and I kept stopping because there were so many bird sounds. At Garrow, which was half way and boasted a few houses, I met some sponsored walkers.

I'd just come down what could be described as a vertical slope and now, one of the poor walkers, who looked quite flaked-out already asked, "Is it steep ahead?" I crossed my fingers behind my back and did not say, "Oh yes, vertical actually," but only "Quite steep," and told them of the beautiful view they would soon be greeted with, which I hoped would soften the forthcoming blow. They were walking from Amulree to Kenmore and I felt very fit and smug because they were younger, without rucksacks, had been walking the flat half and looked exhausted already.

The flat half that I was now on was quite boring and it got colder. I stopped at tea-rooms, just before the Hotel I would be staying at. Linda and Hamish had rung ahead for me and booked that.

There were some bikers from Glasgow at the tea-rooms. One asked for a scone, without cream or jam and his friend said, "He's a hard man," which made me burst out laughing. So, after that, we had a really nice chat. I could just about understand Glaswegian. They said there were lots of English people moved up to the Highlands now. The owners of the tea-rooms bore this out, because they were from Hertfordshire.

As I left, I thought how good it was that my grey hair and obvious age had given me the freedom to chat with young men in friendliness. There was none of the male/female games that were likely to have been played if I had been a young thing. I probably reminded them of their Mums.

The Hotel was very pleasant indeed, with beautiful pictures on the walls everywhere. The owners were from Suffolk. I can hardly ever even think of staying in a Hotel, because the cost is usually well above my budget. If this one had been down in the South, I'm sure I would have had to walk straight by and sleep in a hedge instead but this one was at B & B price and did a very good meal too.

After a very good dinner, I visited the old and small church. It felt very peaceful inside the Church so I stayed there a while and then came back to the Hotel where I talked with a couple who had just moved up here four weeks ago from Essex. I also talked to a grand old gentleman who had actually lived there for 70 years.

Amulree is 1,000 ft. above sea level and is close to the geographical centre of Scotland. The name comes from Maolrubha, which means Mae's Ford in Gaelic. Mae was one of Columba's monks about 650AD. There's that Columba again. He got around.

The place was also one of the oldest cattle trysts in the country. Now, in modern times, it was very quiet there, seemingly in the middle of nowhere, but in those days, there would have been lots of noise as huge herds were driven and got ready for sale. The road I had taken over the hills was one of the old drovers' roads. After sale, the animals would have been driven through Sma' Glen, with up to 30,000 of the beasts being gathered together in fields around Crieff. The drovers ate oatmeal, mixed with some blood taken from the cattle and, when the roads became hard surfaced, the cattle were shod.

At breakfast, I talked to a man in environmental work, who was checking the numbers of black grouse. He had been out since 4 am. I wondered how he managed to get them to stand still long enough count them and he explained about 'Leks' where the grouse gather together for their mating displays. The grouse use the same Leks for hundreds of years. It's like meeting up regularly at a dance floor.

"Hello Cynthia. Here we are again then. I wonder what the fellas have on offer this year? Oh look, that one's got some fine feathers on him. Ah, there's old Fred, trying hard, but doesn't stand a chance, poor old thing. Wow! Look at that one. What a poser!"

There was a post office at the tea-rooms, so I got some money out. That had been a really good idea, to put money in a Post Office Account. It is much easier to get to a Post Office than a Bank, because some of the villages have them and I was walking through villages, but not so many towns.

I was just past the post office, when I realised I hadn't got my compass, which was really serious. I reversed back to the Hotel. The post office let me leave the rucksack there, which made it easier.

At the Hotel, I searched the room I had occupied without success, but just as I was giving up, remembered I'd gone into the bathroom for a shower first thing when I arrived. And there was my precious compass, on a window ledge, behind a curtain, which was just where I had put it.

That was really a lesson against getting careless and not being methodical. Usually, every time I went into a room where I was sleeping, I put my compass, water bottle, maps etc. in a place together. This time, I'd not taken the compass off first before going into the bathroom and was too lazy to take it back to the bedroom and place it where it should be before having a shower. That was a bad mistake. The laziness had cost me a lot more energy and effort having to come back for the compass and the experience cautioned me against breaking from routine in the future.

Anyway, the outcome could have been a lot worse because I had not got very far. It was a bit embarrassing though, having made all the farewells, to suddenly reappear again, all flustered.

On the road once more, I passed through Sma' Glen – the same way as all those animals had been herded and the same way as Malcom the Third had marched to recover his Kingdom from Macbeth. Later, Bonnie Prince Charlie marched through, on his way to the massacre at Culloden. There were dramatic and very high hills rearing up on either side of the pass. I thought of those men, marching through here, on their way to fight. There could have been more than deer looking down at them, waiting to swoop. I bet they felt a bit uneasy.

There was a wild feel to the place now, but then, it would have been very wild indeed, with difficult terrain. I don't expect it was easy walking for those men. The track would have been narrow and rough and they would have known that it could be a walk towards agony and death. They must have really had to hate and want revenge, or be desperate for a job. How good it was to be walking without any feelings of hatred and revenge – just for pleasure. All that hate over all those long years. It doesn't make any sense.

Soon, the scenery changed to more mellow, with hills and farmland looking like a huge country estate, which it may well have been.

I came across a sheep that had stuck her silly head through a square of wire fence, but she had curved horns that stopped her being able to pull her head out again.

Her lamb stood nearby, bleating in distress.

This time, I thought I should interfere, so took hold of the horns, like I was riding a rodeo bull and managed to twist and pull the sheep's head enough for her to pull out but not enough to pull her head off. Mother and child disappeared into the distance rapidly, without even a "thankyou". Perhaps they could smell the mint sauce.

I noticed other sheep pushing their heads through, but nobody else had got stuck. There was plenty of good grass to graze on their side of the fence, yet they just had to push their heads through so that they could get to the grass on the other side, which of course, must be better. Cattle do that too because once, we had a cow that broke down a whole gate which had been separating her from the lush field of grass she was already in, from where there was just one tuft of grass growing in concrete on the other side.

Both animals and people seem to have this 'grass is greener on the other side', so hopefully, there's not an alien species, living on a beautiful planet, but looking at us and saying "Hmm. Now there's a desirable blue planet…"

It had been really cold all day, but suddenly I walked into a fertile plain and it was sunny and warm. Growing in the fields was the first oil seed rape I'd seen since the plane flight. Some of these fields would have been the ones all those animals were driven to from Amulree. How strange this brilliant yellow of the rape would have looked to the people then. It still looks sort of alien to me. The yellow doesn't seem quite the right shade somehow, but it has its own beauty and anyway, is here now and will probably stay.

I got in early to Crieff and drifted round the very pleasant town, having tea and cakes and buying a new water bottle. Then I found very good accommodation and it felt good.

Once I had settled in, I suddenly felt very tired indeed but, next day, my energy had returned and I walked on, to Muthill. I was chided for pronouncing it Mut-hill, just like an ignorant American, thinking it was pronounced the same way as it was spelt. No, it is pronounced Moo-thill. Anybody knows that, like Cirencester is pronounced Sissester.

There were the remains of an ancient church at Muthill and I spent some time there, because it was so fascinating. I read a gravestone for an Agnes, who was born 1742 and died in 1812.

"A lady who discharged the active duties of life with great propriety and died in the hope of a blessed immortality."

I hoped that Agnes' hopes had come true, that there had proved to be a blessed immortality for her, in appreciation of her great propriety. What a waste of all that effort if there wasn't. All that good behaviour and propriety, when she could have been letting rip and having a knees-up. And what if it was true and her hopes were fulfilled? Was the reward yet more expectations of proper behaviour, just politely playing a harp and smiling sweetly at people? That doesn't sound like much fun, not worth all the effort really.

Another stone stated that the husband lived to 92 and the wife to 101, but a son had died at 12 and a daughter at 20, which seemed a bit sad. Maybe they had other children. They had had plenty of time.

It was beautiful, beautiful weather, with blue sky and sunshine, yet cool. I walked on a small and delightful road to Braco. The trees were wearing their best new leaves and the road ahead was dappled sunshine and shade. A helicopter flew low overhead and circled, but didn't shoot.

I had some soup in a pub at Braco. With the choice of two routes, the landlord assured me that the 'B' road to Dunblane had very little traffic so, thinking that it would be a good distance to walk and stop overnight, I took that way. I rather fancied seeing Dunblane Cathedral.

The choice of walking the 'B' road was a good one. The nearby A9 took a shorter and straighter route, but also took all the traffic.

I could see no B & Bs as I walked into Dunblane. The Information Office assured me that there were plenty at Bridge of Allan, which had been my alternative route, so I began to regret my choice, but then, all came right. The lady at the info. gave me the name of one and, although the way to it was a bit of a walk backtracking, it proved to be well worth the effort.

It was a rambling old house, very homely and Grace gave me a large mug of tea straight away, which is the one certain way to become my best friend. There was a beautiful black Labrador, Ivy, who welcomed me with much open paws. Grace told me how to cut through to the Cathedral over and along the river and that there was an organ exhibition at the hall there.

It was a wide and beautiful river, rushing over rocks. The cathedral was about to close, but they let me in and I managed to have a short look around and to admire its magnificent windows, then I visited the organ exhibition. That was fun. I had a go at playing one huge organ and it was a bit like sitting at the controls of a Boeing 707, which of course, I have done so often that I know just what it's like. There were so many keys, knobs and buttons. I swear there was an ejector seat.

I went to buy some fish and chips and sat in the sun to eat them, then back to the church hall for coffee and biscuits. They wouldn't take any money. It was a gift given with warmth and smiles.

As I had come into Dunblane, I had tried not to think about it, tried to give it a chance just to be Dunblane, with its own character, cathedral and beauty, but ahead of me, were four skipping, laughing little girls. The girls were the age of some of the poor little victims of the maniac who, not so very long before, had gunned down so many innocents at their school.

Being here was so different from goggling at news on the box and tutting sadly at the atrocity. I could feel the terrible numbing shock it must have been, the disbelief and horror as the news spread.

And now? Well, I could feel that the shock was still there underneath. People were carrying on, but there was just that slight 'downness' underneath their bravery and friendliness. It will take a long time. Dunblane deserved better.   I liked it very much and was pleased I had come.

* * *

Stirling!   This was a real landmark on my travels. I had not been looking forward to the road walk there, but I had been given directions by my hosts for the Darn Walk, which was not a darn walk at all, but very pleasant and a short cut to Allan Bridge by the river, through woods and countryside. It was another beautiful day of sun and blue sky and I walked into Stirling by noon, with the rest of the day to spend as a tourist.

I booked into the Youth Hostel, which was up a very steep hill, close to Stirling Castle. The Hostel was a very old building next to the old Jail. After booking in and leaving the heavy stuff, I tripped off unladen and carefree to have a look around the Castle.

There were fantastic views from this Castle. I thought of my sister and her son, who had come here when he was young and, in my mind, I could almost see my nephew running around, climbing clambery places, as he would have done then and most likely would do now, come to that!

It was all mixed up with the inevitable history of all that fighting again but then, I suppose it wouldn't have been built at all except for the violence. I wondered how differently towns would have evolved if people had not always fought or had to defend themselves.

I went back to the Youth Hostel and had another indulgence of being able to wash all my clothes. I had a drink of water. I had noticed that water tasted differently in different places. Sometimes, it had been brown with peat but tasted good. Sometimes it had been brown without peat and I didn't like to think about why. In

Stirling, it tasted sharp and metallic, but not of iron.

Off I went then, down town for a meal. There, I noticed an interesting fact. Telephone boxes were never alone, they were always in pairs. Sometimes, they were even in a block of fours. I came across a place where there were two lots of blocks of fours, right next to each other and a pair of large letter boxes, with a postman emptying one of them. I wondered whether all those boxes gathered together for safety, or if they bred here. Maybe that was where all the telephone and letter boxes in the country came from. They had to come from somewhere. Probably, they divide like amoebas.

I picked a phone box at random from the large choice set out in front of me and phoned home. Whilst in there, a fire engine arrived and the firemen gathered in a group just outside. I shot out of the phone box like a rocket, ready to evacuate the area quickly. This was because, the last time I was in London, there was a bomb scare and we all had to squeeze into the Ladies. That was the women anyway, the men squeezed respectfully into the Gents. The day after, in one of the places where my daughter and I had walked, a bomb had exploded, injuring people. So, it was not surprising that I was understandably nervous.

"Is it a bomb scare?" I asked one of the firemen. They all roared with laughter.

"None of that up here," they said.

I enjoyed my stay in Stirling.

At breakfast the next day, I talked to an Australian couple who were off to my part of Sussex and wanted details of National Trust properties, which I was happy to give them. There were quite a few of these around near where I lived and It made me think of how beautiful it was there and what varied scenery there was all around. It was beautiful here all right, but while I was really enjoying what I saw, it made me appreciate too what I had on my own doorstep at home.

Later, as I walked along, I thought of my son and daughter-in-law, who were flying out to Portugal that day. Next time they took a holiday, it would be with another member of the family – my new grand person. I thought of them with love and hoped they'd have a brilliant time, because they both deserved it so much.

It is often the most difficult part of a walk when you have to get out of a big town and on to the right road, but today, I managed it OK without going astray.

The countryside became flattish, very green and fertile, with small, small roads. The smells were familiar to those I was used to in the South – a mixture of nettles and cow parsley but the birds were different here. The day had a dreamy feel and I was very happy, plodding along in the sun, sitting around a bit.

I could hear the sound of a motorway nearby. That was also familiar. I used to resent that sound, but now I treat it as though it were a modern type of waterfall, just a background noise. I can't do anything about it anyway, although I think that in 100 years, it will be silent again, either through different types of transport or none at all. History will probably look back at this period as having been a very noisy time.

It was not so easy finding my way to Bonnybridge. I got lost because roads had been altered and think I went by a very long and boring roundabout route. I finally found what I thought must be the centre of Bonnybridge and had a meal at a café, where different people puzzled over my map, but nobody could read it. They directed me vaguely in the right direction, and that was good enough, because I used my own judgement and found the small road I wanted. This road soon became a track.

The track led past the Antonine Wall, which was a smaller version of Hadrians Wall, but further inside Scotland. There was not much of it left, only mounds, but I wandered over the uneven ground a bit and tried to imagine how it had been in Roman times.

I passed Rough Castle where coal had been mined in an open cast way until 1996. Now, 222 acres had been restored to agricultural use and community woodland.

It was quite a rough track now and I was beginning to get tired. I could have gone on to Falkirk, which was about another three miles but, just off to my right, I saw a barn, on top of a hill, amongst ruins of what must have once been the farm. "Oh ho!" I thought, "This looks promising."

And so it was. In the barn was a nice big trailer, not sloping too much. That made a good, clean wooden surface above ground, which would be warmer than sleeping on the earth. The barn was enclosed, except for the front. It was just about perfect, so I set up home, on the trailer, then had a look around.

The buildings were collapsing, with rubble surrounding them. Once, it must have been a really bustling place up here, but now I could see it wasn't much used for anything because even the trailer had seen better days.

I had a marvellous view all around. In one direction, Falkirk was spread out before me, in another, I could see the hills behind Stirling. I sat happily in the setting sun and brought all the people I loved into my mind. I visualised my dear son, wife and child-to-be in Portugal and they were smiling and happy. I surrounded them in light, to give them a good holiday. Then, I thought of all my other loved ones.

While I sat, I thought, "All the things I've done, the thoughts I've had, the emotions that have made me happy or sad," and it seemed they were all blowing on the wind and away, not of any solid stuff, not mattering, but the feeling was a good one.

My loved ones.

We are like fallen leaves

Taken with the wind

and thrown together

To rest awhile

In a time and place

Until that wind,

tears us one by one

and flutters us away

to different points in space

Then – hurling us

with other leaves

Our loved ones yet unknown.

I felt a great lightness and hoped I would
remember that feeling, but it wasn't solid either, so I knew
I wouldn't be able to hold on to it and it blew away in the
wind as well.

* * *

It was cold, although not so much as previous times so I didn't sleep much. The wind got up in the night and it was very noisy, with bits of the corrugated iron on the barn flapping about. When it was dark, I looked down at Falkirk and was fascinated by bright lights streaming up into the sky. For the shipping I supposed.

I got up at 4.30, made a hot drink and sat watching the sun appear. It rose in the middle of an indentation in the hills and looked for all the world like the cone of a volcano erupting. Then, the sun was snuffed out by heavy cloud and it started raining. Hard and unremitting rain, sloshing down.

I put the trusty umbrella up, which was already minus a spoke, but the wind was very strong and immediately blew it inside out. Then, the umbrella disintegrated into a jumbled and twisted collection of spokes and nylon, so I tucked it untidily into my belt for a funeral later.

The track I was on soon diverged into a bewildering choice, so I took the one I thought most likely. It came out on to a small road, with another track immediately opposite, which was how it looked on the map, but there was such a number of these tracks that it could have been any one of several. Anyway, it must have been the wrong one, for it soon petered out into a footpath, which was very wet, with long grass. Then the footpath completely disappeared into 'moss', which means tussocky bog. By this time, my trainers had been full of water for a while anyway, the footpath was nowhere to be seen and I was lost, with no idea of where I was, so I just sloshed through wherever I could walk without breaking a leg, following the compass.

Somewhere along the way, the wind had removed the waterproof cover to my rucksack and taken it to distant places in Norway, but I didn't even notice that until later. After much swearing and muttering, I got to the road that led to Slammanan and decided against any more tracks and that I would walk down the road, even though it added about three miles to what I should have done.

It was a busy and dangerous road I tramped down now, made even worse by blinding and torrential horizontal rain. I stopped at a bus shelter for a while and it was a relief to be out of the wind and rain. Some people came into the shelter for the legitimate purpose of catching a bus whilst I was in the process of emptying my trainers of water and wringing out my socks. I forced my frozen lips into a smile and said 'hello' but they looked sideways at me in a somewhat nervous way, so I put the wrung out socks and empties trainers back on and departed. It was cold sitting still anyway.

Now, I had rejoined my originally planned route on a blissfully peaceful small road. I was walking along a ridge which was exposed in all directions, with no sheltering trees. At times the wind, which was coming diagonally at me, blew me right across the road. It was a steady force, so that I had to lean over against it, but suddenly, a gust would use my rucksack like a sail and push me right across. Sometimes, as I was leaning against the wind, it would decide to drop for a moment, when I'd have nothing left to lean on and almost fall over. It had an evil sense of humour that wind.

I absolutely hate getting wet, but by this time had accepted sullenly that today, I was going to be very, very wet.

I came to Blackridge, which had a sign announcing proudly that it was a handgun free village, but didn't say anything about gales and found a café where the people were very friendly. I just sort of blew in and, after initial surprise, the ladies in there chatted happily to me.

I was wanting to go on to Harthill, the next village along. The ladies didn't think there was a B & B there, but said to ask when I arrived, which I did and there was. It was the Doxy Hotel, reasonable in price and welcoming. I was very grateful to be there. It was only 2 pm but I'd been walking from 6am and had had quite enough battling against the gale and torrential rain.

The radiator in my room was on, so I had plenty of time now to get everything dry and organised again. Without the protective cover, the water had invaded my rucksack. Luckily the maps were OK, but I had to hang my money up to dry. One of the first things I did was to cut my toenails because, having walked with my feet in water all day, they would never be softer and easier to cut.

I had felt It was very sad, this area and villages. The main employment used to be in open-cast coal mines, which all closed a few years ago. Then, there had been British Leyland and a crisp factory to work for, but they closed too. It's not a tourist area either and farming is hard. Many shops were boarded up and houses empty.

There was very bad reception for the TV, so I couldn't use it. All along my way, when I had been in B & Bs with televisions, I'd noticed the screens had been speckled, showing beautiful background radiation pouring in from the Universe, but useless for anything more local.

I went downstairs to sit and wait for my meal. The bar was full of men, who eyed me askance and I sat at a table alone, feeling awkward. I couldn't even earwig on the conversations, because I found it difficult to understand what they were saying. After a while, I noticed another room, so went in and there were just a couple of ladies which felt better. I think that perhaps up here the villages still kept to the old ways of ladies in one room and men in another and I had not realised that. Whether that was so or not, I felt more comfortable anyway and the landlord brought my meal, which he had done specially for me because they didn't do meals that evening. That was very kind of him, I appreciated it a great deal and there were lots of vegetables which I especially enjoyed because I don't get so many of them along the way when I'm walking.

It was a bit smoky in my room at night because the bar was underneath and the smoke seeped up through the floor but, after all, it was a pub and who was I to deny the local people their pleasures in what seemed to be a tough enough life. Listening to the wind, blowing wildly outside, I was very grateful to have the comfort of my room, because now, it had turned cold enough to snow. I could have been looking for another barn in the cold wind and rain instead of being snug and warm.

Looking to the days ahead, I felt a bit 'down' because I could see it might be hard to get accommodation and the weather had turned so bad. There might not be many places to buy food either if I had to sleep out, but I decided that I wouldn't worry about it now, but trust to the usual pattern of it being all right in the end. After all, the weather had changed so rapidly from beautiful to atrocious, that I supposed it could do it the other way around.

I had originally planned a bit of footpath walking in this area but now, because of the weather, I realised I would have to alter it to road walking. It was not as I had wanted but then, is anything? Even on the busier roads though, I could get a good taste of the countryside surrounding me.

Next morning, the weather looked horrible and it was only a small place I was heading for. Suddenly, I felt a bit insecure and supposed it was a reaction to having been going for three weeks and thought that I'd done the hardest bit, through the mountains, but today and next week looked like it could be harder still. It seemed to be taking a long time to walk through Scotland.

Talking to the landlady that morning, she told me of the stress she had been under for the last 10 years. Everywhere I go, however idyllic the surroundings, people seem to have their problems but here, in this area, the whole background was stress. She told me that 'Orange Marchers' are very strong here. The area is actually nicknamed 'Little Ulster'. How could I blame the people for being angry? In comparison to their hard lives, here was I, just walking, without any cares other than immediate purely physical ones of aching muscles and finding somewhere to sleep. I was also aware that I was walking for fun, playing a game, with a good home to go back to whenever I wanted, but for so many people in the world, there was no secure and comfortable home and the game they were playing was to keep themselves and their loved ones alive. That would not be fun at all. When I paid for my meal and accommodation, I noticed that I had not been charged for a drink the previous evening. I told the landlady of this and she just smiled and said 'Have it on us'. That was so typical of some people who don't have so very much themselves but are so generous.

With that kindness and, once I got into my stride, I felt better. After all, hadn't everything turned out well so far? The wind was as strong as ever but improved as the day went on, with some sun in between squalls of rain. It gave way to more sun than squalls, but still very cold. I could see old mines and heaps of waste all around, but lots of the land was being reclaimed and areas of trees were growing up. Before the replanting, it must have been a desolate moonscape indeed.

I walked against the West wind for a while. What silly fool would choose to do the walk this way, into the facing wind? It was terrible, like pushing hard all the time against a great heavy weight. I got very angry at the wind and shouted abuse at it, but it didn't take a blind bit of notice. After a while, I turned southeast, so at least I was being pushed sideways.

Nature compelled me to stop along the way and

seek an isolated bush, suitable for a woman. Then, I couldn't believe it! As soon as my pants were down, a car drew up and a couple with a dog got out. The dog bounced over with great enthusiasm and interest.

Up until now, it had puzzled me that, when I stopped for such a personal purpose, however isolated and hidden the spot, in a higher than would be expected number of times, somebody would arrive on the scene. Now though, looking at the car, I believed I understood why. I noticed the car registration included the letters VGA. Of course! That must be the code for VEGA. All these people, who seem to arrive out of nowhere by chance, must be from a planet near the star Vega, sent to earth to observe us humans in such local customs as I had just been performing. Now I understood, I smiled cheerily at the people as they passed by.

On the road again, the car passed and gave me a friendly toot. They probably think I'm one of them.

I sallied forth to Forth, and noticed that there were a lot of shops shut up and boarded. These mining villages I was passing through seemed to have been built in strings of houses, strung out along the road in a line. I could see this clearly when approaching or looking back at them. They were not built around a centre, or in a cluster like most villages. I suppose they were built by the landlords in an easy and functional way, rather than thinking of the places as a community.

I noticed also, while walking along that many trees had been uprooted not so long ago. There must have been a pretty strong wind to do that, more like a hurricane.

I had asked whether the gale I was experiencing was unusual and was told that it was pretty normal to have strong winds around there. 'Strong' seemed to me to be a bit of an understatement. Heavens above – if this wind had only been 'strong' what would 'severe' be like?

Walking about 16 miles, I got to Carnwath where I caught a small bakers that was just about to shut and got myself a take-away cup of tea and roll. I sat in the shelter of a car repairer's yard to consume them.

I may have stopped for the night, but I only saw one place and, looking at it, preferred the open moor. It was only 3.00 and I felt quite lively, so decided to go on to Biggar, even though it was another 7 miles.

I did all right until the last 3 miles, when I suddenly began to feel more tired. It started raining then. When I still had 2 miles to go, trudging along in the rain, there was a very kind happening. A man and lady in a van stopped to offer me a lift. It was very tempting, but I was a good girl and explained why I couldn't take up their offer. They accepted the explanation with amusement but then, they said "Well, perhaps you'd like a cup of tea and piece of cake?" There was absolutely no "perhaps" about it!

The couple had come from Birmingham to stay away for the weekend, but their holiday had been cut short when the lady had become quite ill, perhaps from eating something bad. I thought it was all the more kind of them, when having problems of their own, to think of my comfort.

That pleasant experience made me glow and got my feet flying the remaining 2 miles. I soon found a good B & B at Biggar and food shops as well.

I phoned home, to hear that they had been worried about me because they had heard there were 60 mph gales up here. I told them that 60 mph was no exaggeration and dramatised satisfactorily what I had walked through. The forecast was for some improvement, and indeed, the wind had already eased a bit.

I liked Biggar very much. It is an ancient settlement, with stone-age habitations and burial sites on Biggar Common. Of course, the Romans had been here. They got everywhere.

William Wallace defeated the English army here in 1297. He had disguised himself as a pedlar to spy on the enemy camp and probably made himself a few bob, selling souvenirs to the English.

Here, on the last night of every year, even today, the roads are all shut and a huge bonfire is lit in the high street. This has been done for thousands of years (probably originally on the shortest day), to burn the old year out and give heat to encourage the sun to come back. During the war, when there was the blackout ruling, they still made the symbolic gesture with a few locals burning some bits of wood at the bottom of a tin can.

I thought of how important it had once been, this ceremony to encourage the sun to come back. We live now with the knowledge that our British days will get shorter and shorter until mid-winter solstice and then get longer again. Because we know the reasons for it, we are confidently sure and don't even think of worrying. But imagine how it used to be. Every year, it happened that the days had got longer every day, with the sun busily working up there. Then, the sun started to get a bit tired and didn't stay up quite as long. The poor old sun got even more tired and spent more time in bed. The days got shorter and shorter.

People would have noticed that this happened every year. As the days continued to get shorter, the sun would set slightly more to the left every night and rise more to the right every morning until, on a certain day, seen from a certain place, it would rise perhaps in between two hills, or some other marker.

In previous years, the sun had not risen the following day past that marker but had risen ever so slightly to the left of the marker and then, the people would know that everything was going to be all right, that the sun was going to get strong again, that the days would get longer, that summer would come.

You couldn't rely on it though. You couldn't be sure. Perhaps one year, the poor old sun would be so tired that it wouldn't be able to recover and the days would carry on getting shorter until the sun died completely and it would always be night. That would be bad news.

So, as the solstice drew near, it was quite a worrying time. Ways of encouraging and nourishing the sun had to be found. Sacrifices may have to be made. Even then, you could never be quite sure. Imagine the tension on the morning that the big decision was to be made. Would the sun rise just to the left of where it had risen the day before? Or would the sun rise to the right, heralding an even shorter day and a possible descent into eternal darkness? Would it be 'all go' for another year?

What relief and jubilation there would have been, when dear old sol did its job (if of course you could see the damn thing for clouds). What celebrations and junketings would have taken place. A knees-up like that would have been something to look forward to during the long winter.

No wonder the celebration of mid-winter solstice was a British festival that the new Christian movement could not dare to break, so they cunningly moved the celebration on a few days and called it Christmas. It was a clever move.

Anyway, now we think we're confident of the sun's behaviour and satisfactorily in charge of the whole planet well enough not to have to find the odd virgin to sacrifice. Just as well really. Virgins are getting a bit hard to come by.

Now I was entering the Border country. It was beautiful. I phoned my ex husband, as I often did, because we are good friends. He told me some sad news, that our dog Poppy had had a stroke and that it would have been cruel to let her live like that. My daughter had gone to the farm to be with him and Poppy and they both took her to the vet in his van. That would have pleased her because she always used to jump in the van hopefully as soon as the door was opened. The vet came out to the van and Poppy smiled up at him and died without fear or distress.

It had been the right decision, easily made for a dog, although we choose to let humans carry on longer and suffer. I was so pleased that my daughter had been with husband. They buried Poppy and then had a funeral pyre of her box and blankets with the flames being a celebration of her life. She was over 14 and had had a good old life of freedom on a farm. Still, I was sad, because you are sad when someone you love dies, so I sat in the shelter of an old wall and cried.

I thought of the young dog and the old dog, which were just the same inside and I thought of all the happy times we'd had as a family together with her.

She was sad when we all went our own ways, but that sadness happens to humans too. Mostly I think, she was happy and Mike had been very kind to her when she became an old lady. Often he had carried her up steps when she found it difficult to get up them.

I thought of a time, firm in my memory, when Poppy and me had both gone for a walk in the snow. I had been a bit worried that her paws were cold, but she said they were OK. We stopped in a glade where a stream flowed. Icicles hung from the rocks, reflecting all the sun's colours and big flakes of snow were falling. I lifted my head, put out my tongue and caught some flakes as they fell. They tasted of nothing – just snow.

I had felt so happy that I had laughed out loud and Poppy had laughed too. We had both stood there, by the stream, laughing together.

Now, I walked on and, for a while, there was a

black dog with me, running around, sniffing all the exciting new smells, young and happy.

I arrived at a Hotel, the only place to stop for many miles. A batch of leather clad bikers had roared by me on the road and I found them gathered in the bar. There was only one girl to serve everybody, so I waited and chatted to the bikers, who were a laugh and thought I was quite nuts using my feet instead of two wheels.

The Hotel was more expensive than a B & B. I don't often stay in Hotels because of the price. When I have done, I often find that they have what I need and are functional but more impersonal and not as warm a feeling as a B & B, which I suppose is inevitable. I always prefer the cosy B & Bs and the interesting people I meet there.

I got the feeling that this Hotel was probably struggling for continued existence, like so many seemed to be. They were managing to hang on, but no extra money for refurbishment.

I got talking to a lovely lady from Tweedsmuir, who was from just down the road and she asked me to tea, so later I went. It was about a mile further on, easy walking without the rucksack and I found the beautiful house high up on a hill. I walked up a path lined with bluebells that were not only blue, but pink and white as well. The house nestled in a setting of wooded hills.

The lady who had invited me was visiting her sister, whose house it was. It was a very large house for one person, but there is plenty of property available up here. There were two young, freshly married Americans there too. The wife was trying to trace her family name, which was the same as the sisters, and a lady from the tourist office had brought them along. They produced a really old book, with a lot of detail about the family in it, which thrilled the Americans.

I very much enjoyed my tea with them all and behaved myself admirably. I resisted the temptation to grab the delicious goodies offered with both hands and stuff the food into my mouth in a circular motion, and took up the cakes delicately, with one hand and a fair amount of moderation.

Later, I had a very good meal at the Hotel and met a lady from Peebles. She also loved walking and we talked a lot and exchanged addresses. She said I'd be welcome to stay with her at any time and I welcomed her to Sussex if ever she wanted. That was one of the really good things about this walk. I was meeting such great people.

* * *

I was now in the Border Country. This was Roman Territory, or what they had tried to make their territory anyway.

I walked along, thinking about all those marching legionaries and hummed a little Roman-type song, imagining that I was there marching with them. Except that I was wearing trainers and not sandals. Once, I used to imagine all those soldiers walking in their sandals and that the sound would be a regimental 'flop flop' as they walked along. Then I saw in a museum that the sandals had had metal studs in the soles, so it would have been a more noisy affair and you'd probably have been able to hear them coming from a long way off.

It was an ancient frontier zone I was walking now. A most beautiful country of hills and woods, but with such a history of hatred - fighting and killing and all for an artificial border, which separated human beings that any alien would regard as indistinguishable from each other.

If we fight each other so much all the time, beware of visiting us, you beings from different worlds. We are all of the same species but are so very involved with killing. We are afraid enough of each other, let alone anybody amongst us who is different at all who we fear even more. You, Mr. Alien, will be very different. You wouldn't stand a chance.

So, listen here you aliens, I have advice for you. If you choose to land on the earth, best that you appear as small and furry, preferably with appealing big eyes. If you are unfortunate enough to have an insect or reptilian-like structure then, even if fantastically peace loving and gentle, bringing the earth people knowledge and a future beyond their wildest dreams – no chance – SPLAT! Welcome to Planet Earth.

I looked at the rocks all around me. Many were formed when the land I was standing on was in the Southern Hemisphere and had a lovely warm climate, about 400 millions years ago, long to me, but young to the earth. Dead volcanoes and Hill Forts were everywhere and, at one time, all around here roamed Euroch (very large cattle), elk, bear, wolves and beavers.

As I was getting further South, the sound of the names was changing. Some still had a Scots twang to them, but now, some were sounding a bit North Country in tone.

I turned off East to the Megget Reservoir. Here, there were two reservoirs and both had flat ends to them. It rang a memory bell. They were just like the ones I had seen from the plane when flying up to Inverness. A plane flew overhead that could have been on route to Inverness so it was highly likely, I thought. Fancy that! It could be that I was actually walking now on land I had looked down on from the plane.

Talking to someone later, they said that the straight ends of the reservoirs were not made by human agency, but were natural formations of the rock.

Violets were around me everywhere. I came across a sign by one of the reservoirs that said "Fly Only - No Swimming". Obviously the Scots were way above the English when it came to personal transport.

I carried on marching with the Legionaries, swinging along with the Eagle at the front, superior in the knowledge that I was a Roman. Soon I got fed up with the same old Roman tune and hummed St.Louis Blues instead, like it was done in the film about Glenn Miller. That was a good marching rhythm. I bet the Romans would have really loved that.

I puffed up a very steep hill and looked down at a marvellous view of wild hills and reservoir. Sheep surveyed me curiously. I looked for the one wearing a red woolly hat, because my ears were cold, but the hat was most likely still up there somewhere in the Highlands.

Then, as I was dragging up another steep hill, something very worrying happened. I felt a sharp and intense pain on the top of my right foot, just in front of the ankle.

Up until then, I had had no trouble at all with the old feet, not a blister or sore spot even. If there ever seemed to be a danger of tenderness, I shoved sheep wool in the shoe at that spot and it soon relieved the tenderness before it got really sore. There was surely a good supply of sheep wool hanging about. I had expected a bit of trouble from my left little toe, which had been broken the year before. A few weeks after it had been broken, I had managed to limp the Thames Path for a week with friends even though it had hurt but, on this walk, the toe had resigned itself to the inevitable and given me no trouble at all.

Now though, the pain crept upwards and the whole of my lower right leg hurt very much.

I changed my trainers, hoping that it would help but then, when it didn't, just carried on walking and hoped that it was a purely temporary affliction and would go again as quickly as it had come. Pains are like that sometimes. They are bad, then they just go.

This pain was determined though and I started to get a bit worried about it. I didn't want anything to stop my walk now.

I was pleased I had made the decision to go by the reservoir road. I had planned originally to cut across the hills the day before by an attractive looking footpath and that would have saved me a whole day's additional walk and given beautiful views. Because of the weather and strong winds, I had decided it was too risky walking that route by myself. It would have taken me up very high and, if I had been blown over and fallen badly, could have been in trouble. Indeed, if the trouble I was now experiencing had happened up there, it could have been less fun than a bowl of custard poured over my head.

I reached Tibbie Shiel Hotel and was very grateful because now, I could stop the pain by stopping walking. I had noticed there were two Hotels here on the map, but the first one wasn't there any more. This one was wonderful - friendly, cosy and warm. It was a very reasonable price too, much to my surprise, because it was in a beautiful situation, right next to St.Mary's Loch. Except for the leg, it was bliss.

I showered and sat looking at the view of the Loch out of my window, with my leg up. I got lovely and warm. Then I had a good meal. Afterwards, I talked with some other guests, two Canadians and another walker, who was walking the Southern Uplands Way. I would be walking a bit of that the next day. It was a happy and companionable evening.

I slept fitfully, because the leg throbbed all night. I kept telling myself that it would be much better in the morning and, when the morning came, there was a black bruise on the front of my shin. It seemed to me that a vein had broken and the blood had travelled up the leg to form the bruise. I reckoned that I could have caused it myself by pulling my laces too tightly because, I was so determined not to get a twisted ankle, I might have overdone the tightening. I cussed myself for being so stupid as to cause myself this unnecessary injury.

Anyway, now that the bruise had come out, I hoped it would get better quickly.

Next day, I walked about five miles on the Southern Upland Way, which was very hilly and very, very beautiful. My trainers were not very suitable for the slippery bits and rough ground, but I was careful and loved being remote and alone for a while.

Alone that is, except when I wanted a 'wee'. There was nobody in sight in any direction. Except for a man with dogs right at the very beginning, I had seen nobody all day. So, I squatted in supposed privacy and security. Upon which, three husky young men appeared as if from nowhere. They were very kind and tactful and immediately turned their backs to admire the view for a while, but we all wore broad grins when we met.

The young men didn't admit to being from Vega. They said they were from Holland and were finding the Southern Uplands Way very tough, because Holland is flat and this countryside most certainly was not. They said there were Bothies to stay at along the Way, so I made a mental note of this for a future walk.

Considering it had been such tough walking, I got along with the leg very well. I told myself that it was only like having a migraine in my leg. I was used to coping with those and this was better because at least the pain was only in one place and the rest of my body didn't feel ill like it did with a migraine.

So the leg was the leg and the rest of my body was well and, either it felt a bit better because of that, or it was getting better. I hoped so. I could cope with pain but, now that I had managed to get away for a long enough time to do this longed for walk, I didn't want to have to give it up for something so silly as a bad leg.

My constant fear had been that I would have to give up some time during the walk and go home if Mum had become ill. I had taken the responsibility for two six week stretches so that I was 'in credit' for a month. I felt almost guilty at times for the relief and happiness I felt at only having to think of myself. After all, we are trained to believe that it's right and proper to be caring for somebody, always putting them first and taking the responsibility and so, we usually do. We often do it for our children and then for our parents and that's life. I was a bit ashamed of myself for how happy I felt at experiencing this freedom but it felt really good.

Walking along, even with the bad leg, I had to admit that I was so easy to be with. There was pulling in me in two ways, one being what I really wanted to do and the other what life dictated I had to do. The problems were very simple – food and survival. No trouble. I was so easy to look after! I even laugh at my own jokes.

After the Southern Uplands Way, I walked past Ettrick. I'd wondered so much, when looking at where I'd be walking, what it was like around here. It had looked such a wild, remote and sparsely populated part of the country. Now, I was finding that it looked like that because it was a wild, remote and sparsely populated part of the country.

I knew where I was heading though. That was, Eskdalemuir. Someone had told me that I would be passing Samye Ling, which was a Tibetan Retreat Centre. I had heard of it because friends had spent some time there and also that they had a tea-room and did B & B.

It would be a 20 mile walk for the day, even more perhaps and with a hurting leg, but I was determined to make it. I wasn't quite sure where Samye Ling was on the map and hoped it was nearer rather than further, but it turned out to be further.

When I had walked a long way and knew I should be getting close, I asked a road-worker if he knew of the place. He did and said it was three miles further on.

I knew that I was going at the speed of about three miles an hour because, by now, I could judge this pretty well. One hour and three miles after the information, there was still no sign of Samye Ling. The road curved in between hills and, every time I rounded a hill, I hoped that I would see some sight of it, but every time, I didn't. I asked a gentleman working in his garage if the place actually existed and, if so, how far was it?

"Three miles," said he.

And he was telling the truth because, about just over that distance later, I dragged myself into Samye Ling and staggered into the office.

"Is the tea-room still open?" I enquired hopefully.

"No, just shut a few minutes ago, but here, you can have my tea, I've not drunk any yet," said a young man who was standing there holding a mug of tea. "You look like you need it," he said with a grin.

I accepted the gift gratefully and was soon laughing and chatting with the people there. I could apparently choose between having a private room to myself, or for less cost, a dormitory. I chose the dorm, not only for the cost, but because I fancied being part of the community rather than shut off from it. A lady came in and said that she was the only other one in with me because there were not many people here at that particular time. She showed me the way then, once I was settled, showed me all around and where the showers were.

I felt very welcome and happy. Frances was very concerned about my leg. Indeed, looking at it now, it was pretty obvious that it had become poisoned and the swelling was inflamed, hot and painful to touch. She made me promise absolutely that I would go to a doctor in Langholm the next day and assured me that somebody would certainly drive me there. I promised I would go to a doctor, but said I was going to walk there rather than be driven because it was on my way.

I did appreciate the care and kindness shown to me. When somebody cares like that about me, I am always very moved and a bit taken aback. It was genuine care here, you can tell. It was a very nice feeling of warm companionship with Frances. She was going off the next day to Holy Island, a little island off the larger island of Arran. This was part of Samye Ling, with a community of monks and retreat facilities there. The island had once been owned by a Catholic Community and there is a painted cave there that has been and still is being used for prayer and meditation. My daughter had stayed for a week and loved it. I had tried to stay there for a week. One November, I had caught the overnight coach from London to Glasgow and over to Arran, but there had been gales and the man who operated the small boat that went from Arran to Holy Island would not go. Who can blame him? I had wandered over Arran a bit, but the Youth Hostels were closed and so was most of everything else. The gales were forecast to carry on a whole week so, together with a few people from Samye Ling and a disgruntled television crew who had been on the way over there to film a documentary, I returned on the last ferry and back to London again. I had never gone back as yet, although intended to one day.

So, at least I had seen the island that Frances was headed for from a distance, so could visualise where she was going for a whole month.

There was a meal provided in the evening and, afterwards, I went to the evening Puja. The shrine room was magnificent. I didn't know the Tibetan chants, but was just happy and very peaceful sitting there listening to the chanting and the Tibetan instruments, which always struck a chord somewhere deep inside me. Then, we meditated and I felt my gratitude at having been safe so far in my journey, with my loved ones all safe and happy too.

The person who went to bed that night intended to get up and go to the 6am Puja, but the person who woke at the correct time, was a completely different one, who rolled over and went back to sleep. Well, the leg pain had caused me a bit of a disturbed night was my excuse.

I should have liked to have stayed another day at Samye Ling, but definitely had to get to the doctor.

Frances went off with some others and I was again offered a lift to Langholm, but knew that I'd be able to walk it OK. It would be about 10 to 15 miles. All my estimates are a bit approximate.

The 'B' road had such little traffic, it was not worth taking the smaller one. It was best too that the walk was as short as possible, because the pain was now quite considerable.

It was a lovely route, with most beautiful scenery. Alternately, I walked through forest, which gave way to open hills capped with forest, then forest again. I loved walking with trees all around me. Once, I walked through an ancient valley. I could feel the ancientness of it and there was a stone circle in one of the fields. People had been around here for a long while and I could just imagine woolly mammoths stomping around at one time. The landscape suited mammoths but, at the time they were around, there would have been a lot more snow and ice.

I met a cyclist who was on the way up to John O'Groats. He was William Hadley from Essex and was raising money for charity. He had already raised enough from other things he had done to buy a whole lifeboat. I felt a bit ashamed that I wasn't using my walk for such a useful purpose.

William was most impressed at my age and the fact that I was doing the walk, when it was obvious that I was well past my 'sell by' date. "Why are you doing it?" he asked. "Haven't you got anything better to do?"

This question was certainly not meant as a criticism or a challenge, it was just a curiosity as to my motives. It made me think for a moment. Hadn't I got anything better to do? No, I decided. I hadn't. There was nothing better at the moment that demanded my attention. There was nothing I would rather be doing.

William took my photo and said he would send me a copy. I should have liked to have taken one of him, but had used up the last in the throw-away camera. I had decided I was not going to carry the weight of a normal camera, but discovered that the throw-aways were so light and small, I could carry one in my pocket, send it home to my sister, with any used maps and then buy a new camera.

I told William about the tea-room at Samye Ling, which he said he would welcome and off we went in opposite directions, he to John O' Groats and me to Land's End. Except that I would be going for a lot longer. It had been a spirit-lifting experience to talk with him, because he was so full of energy and enthusiasm.

It was 3.30 as I walked into Langholm and I found a B & B straight away, where the kind lady there immediately produced a tray of tea and goodies. She told me where there was a doctor. It was not far away, so I showered and went there without delay.

I waited a bit, which was only reasonable and to be expected, as I had arrived out of the blue, then a sweet lady doctor saw me. She said that, yes, the leg had most certainly become poisoned. It was inevitably early closing day so the chemists was closed, but she had antibiotics and so gave me them. So now, I had done the best I could for the suffering limb and it had just got to get on with being a leg and keep on walking.

Langholm was a nice place and friendly. People chatted to me in an easy way and looked happy.

In the morning, I got some more money out of the Post Office and started off for Newcastleton. Then, I suddenly thought about it, stopped, looked at the map and made a decision to change route to cut more diagonally across towards Penrith.

This decision was caused by the fact that my daughter was coming out to walk with me for a week. She had always intended to but now knew the date she could come, which was 30th May. It was now 27th May, so I had to get to Penrith to receive her, which was a deviation from the route I had originally planned. Sticking now to the original route would cause me to walk a much longer distance and maybe have to take a bus into Penrith and back again, which would be rather silly, because on this new route, walking smartly, I could get to Penrith well within the time.

So, I set off in the altered direction, not quite sure of where I was going, but somehow more relaxed. I had put a target on myself of reaching Samye Ling and then had to get to Langholm for the doctor, but now I had no pressure of having to get anywhere particular for the next couple of days. All I had to do was to go a certain distance in a certain direction. That felt fluid and free.

I got all philosophical and thought that life was like this walk really. I had put the stress on myself of having to be somewhere, first by the wish to go to a certain place and second by choosing to walk and not get a lift. I didn't regret either decision but, looking back, I could see that it had caused a certain amount of tension. In life generally, I could understand that I caused myself stresses by my own actions. I decided that it was all right though. If I could learn to see when I was causing myself such stresses, I could go off on a walk and see what I was doing. Then, when I came back, I could either go along with it and enjoy the stresses, or do something else. Another good theory!

It seemed to me that the only time I really got stressed out and unhappy was when I was in a situation beyond my own control. Then I was stuck and could not easily do much about getting unstuck without hurting other people in the process. Perhaps I could learn to see the traps before they came and side-step them. I could try. A person gets a bit philosophical walking by themselves and inevitably a bit self-searching, but it is interesting what comes up in the old mind.

My leg still hurt a lot as I walked along, but that meant I didn't notice sore shoulders any more and hadn't even had to sit on stinging nettles to achieve that.

The animated box had reported that the day would be dry. It was going to be a big day today too. I was going to cross the border!

It was a lovely walk. I could have been walking in the Devon lanes, because it looked like that and smelled like it too. It was mellow and had a humidity that I loved. I don't like it too humid, but when it's just enough so that my face feels damp, well, I love that and feel very healthy.

I phoned Mike. He was having a cup of tea with a farmer friend. The previous time I phoned, he'd been doing the same and I teased him that I thought they spent the day drinking tea together and never did any work. I knew this was not at all true, because they are very hard workers. One day a week, he will go to his friend's and help for a day on the friend's farm. The next week, they'll do a day's work at his farm. When people get together like that, it makes sense, like me and my sister got together with our problem. The mystery is, why people don't do it more often.

I passed Claygate, where I thought I saw a notice saying 'Peasants Crossing' but on closer inspection, it said 'Pheasants Crossing', but I crossed anyway. There was a cuckoo giving forth with a very loud sound. It must have got itself a microphone and speakers.

"Right fellas. One speaker in the oak and the other in the sycamore. Now, is it balanced? I don't want a louder 'cuck' than 'oo', or 'oo' than 'cuck' come to that. Ready? There's a walker coming along now. Ready, set, deep breath – give her a blast!"

There were lots of freshly green trees around. I felt that I was walking among vegetation that was sprouting almost quick enough for me to watch it grow and, when I sat amongst the greenery for a while, I thought that, if I stayed there for too long, it might grow all around and engulf me.

That didn't seem such a bad thought - to become part of the greenery. Sometimes, as I sit amongst growing things, I feel part of them anyway. Perhaps, when I die, my family could sneak my body away to a green and lush wood, where it would become part of the surroundings and feed the little creatures. But then, it wouldn't be allowed. I had learned at some time that nobody could dispute what a person had instructed should happen to their money, if they had made a Will but, if they put in what they wanted done with their body, even if it was an officially allowed thing, other people could disagree and do something completely different if they chose. The money instruction is binding, but the body one is not. So – your money seems to be considered much more important than poor old you.

At last! Here I was, crossing the river Liddel Water, which marked the Border. There was nothing else there. No sign saying "Well done, Pat, what a fantastic walk! Have a haggis." Much to my disgust, there wasn't even a sign saying 'Welcome to England.' I'd been looking forward to taking a photo of that because, despite the lack of welcoming committee, this was a big event in my walk. I reckoned that, even though Scotland was one third of the distance on the map, in actual distance walked and effort, it was more like a half.

I could see that there had been a sign, but someone, no doubt Scots Independence enthusiasts, had ripped it down. Well, now they had won independence, so they could just put it back again. I turned round and there was a sign, bold and whole, saying 'Welcome to Scotland. So I had to take a photo of that instead and pretend that I was walking backwards.

I hung over the middle of the bridge for a while to see what it felt like to be suspended between Scotland and England, but it didn't feel any different, so I walked on triumphantly and entered the country of my birth. I must admit though that my experience of Scotland had been beautiful scenery and real kindness from just about everybody I had met.

* * *

I was now walking in the middle of the 'Disputed Lands'. It couldn't have been very secure living here. If you were an innocent family trying merely to live in peace and get a living from the land, first you could be zapped by tribesmen from the North rampaging South or, as an attractive alternative, zapped by people from the South rampaging North.

If I had been them, I would have had a collection of badges to wear depending on who was around at the time, saying, "Up the Picts", "Up the Brits", "Up the Romans", or even, in defiance and to be worn in private, "Up Yours."

A bit dodgy, life had been in the Borders though. It couldn't have been a popular choice to live here. I'll bet property was cheap. It still wasn't very densely populated even now.

A bit to the South of me was Gretna Green. That was a popular place when I was young, because couples under 21 had to get parental permission in England to be married, but the legal age for marriage was younger in Scotland, so eager couples used to elope up to Gretna. It used to be considered a very romantic thing to do. Different laws are in operation now though, so it's no longer necessary but I think some couples still choose to go their to tie the knot but still, they must have lost a lot of custom.

It was brewing up for a storm that night and threatened to be very wet indeed. I was heading for a lovely sounding place called 'Beyond the Moss'. At least it was 'beyond' and not 'in'. I'd had enough of being 'in the moss'. It did give an indication of what the ground was like though.

Suddenly, a very large hare rushed out on to the road in front of me. It sat up startled and stationary with fear and surprise for a short while. I had never seen a hare so close up before. It had round blobs on the ends of its very large ears. Then, it came to its senses and dashed into the adjoining field, where it ran to a safe distance and sat up again, watching me go by.

I sat in a woodland clearing, with sweet smells wafting over me. There were sounds of the curlew all around. One plant that looked like lavender didn't smell so sweet. It smelled more like dog's poo.

I came to an Inn and thought, great – tea perhaps, but no chance. I tried all the doors, but they were firmly shut. Nobody was around. Then a lady called Caroline stopped her car to see if I was lost. We chatted and she said her friend Jane ran the Post Office at Catlowdy and it was the only shop for miles, so if I wanted provisions, I'd best call there.

When I got to the Post Office, I bought some food, then asked Jane if there was any accommodation nearby.

"You can stay here if you don't mind a folding bed in the children's play room," she said.

I said that it sounded like luxury to me and that I had my own bedding. Then started such a pleasant stay.

Jane ran the Post Office, which was open three days a week. Her husband, Will, was in the airforce, but not far away, so he was home every night and they had two beautiful children, Andrew 5 years old and Katrina 3.

I played with the children in the garden and was frustrated that I couldn't run after a frisbee very well, because of the leg. Normally, I'd have belted along after it and wouldn't have let Andrew win like he did!

There seemed to be so much to learn to run a Post Office. I was able to help in a very small way by sticking stamps on a pile of parcels, which made me feel very important. Postman Pat!

I very much enjoyed being with this lovely family. The children reminded me of mine when they were the same age and it was a while since I'd been in the company of such little ones. It was giving me good practice for my forthcoming grandparenthood.

Talking that night, I learned some very interesting things. Catlowdy is near enough to the border to choose between English or Scots schools, but Jane and Will thought that Scots schools were better. You get fined £50 if you shoot a white pheasant, because they can be seen clearly when they are roosting. If they are not to be seen then it could be a warning that there were poachers around.

English and Scots fishing laws are different. You need a licence to fish in English waters, but not Scots. On the border river I'd walked over, everybody naturally fishes on the Scots side.

In the morning, Jane made me a substantial lunch box full of goodies and she wouldn't take anything at all for putting me up and feeding me. She said, "Would you charge me if I stayed with you" and I had to admit that I wouldn't, so she said "Well then!" So, I accepted the kindness and generosity given to me and hoped that I could show the same to somebody in my turn.

I did find out that the children liked Winnie the Pooh and formed the intention to call in at the Winnie the Pooh shop when I got back home, because Winnie lives very near to us on the Ashdown Forest. I know him well and we have many chats on my walks on the Forest. Sometimes, in the rain, he mistakes me for Eeyore. Visiting the shop would give me a good excuse to browse around it anyway. I love doing that and can't wait until my grandchild is old enough to play with the same toys that I fancy playing with.

It was absolutely tipping it down outside, with hardly a space between the raindrops and thunder and lightning too. It would have been grim if I had had to sleep outside overnight. I should have been pretty wet and miserable by now so I was so very grateful to Jane for her kindness.

Jane had to go out and said for me to wait a while to see if it eased off and showed me where to leave the key. She had such complete trust in me, a stranger.

The thunder and lightning stopped, but the rain looked like it would be carrying on for a long while yet, so I resigned myself and launched out.

It was surely heavy rain and an absolute network of little roads, clear on the map, but not when I was walking them. There were names of houses and farms on the map, so I could have found out where I was easily enough, except for something I had noticed with irritation before. That was - very few people where I had been walking seemed to put up the names of their houses. Such names seemed to be a well-kept secret and I pitied any new postman.

There was a point today at which, if only the large house on the corner had had its name up, it would have been certain which road to take. But the house did not display its name. It wasn't about to divulge such personal and secret local knowledge to a dripping wet backpacker. I even knocked on the door to ask, but either there was nobody home, or they were hiding behind the curtains giggling. So, I sheltered in a shed for a while for a bit of relief from the rain and then made a choice. It turned out to be the wrong one and, for a while, I got not exactly lost, but a bit mislaid.

I picked up a road then that led in a pretty direct manner to Brampton. A small road, smelling all the way of sweet cow parsley which brought back memories of my childhood during the Wartime years spent in Devon. I don't know why it is, but smells smelled in childhood seem to be fixed in the mind forever and a flash of them brings back a host of memories. Often, walking down such lanes, I am a little girl again, without the cares of being a grown-up, except that I can see over the hedges a bit better now. They used to be much higher.

The rain was pretty constant and very heavy, but at least it was vertical and the temperature was warm, so it could have been worse.

Along the way, a Doberman dog came up and barked at me. I put my hand on my dog 'scarer', ready to use it if necessary.

I have rarely had to use this doggy deterrent but once, I had to negotiate my way through the caravans of a travelling fairground, because they were right in front of a right-of-way I was looking for. An Alsatian leaped out and took hold of my trouser leg, but I stopped, got the 'scarer' out of my pocket, pointed it at the dog and gave a short burst. It ran off and wouldn't come near me again. The object emits a very high pitched sound that is painful to dogs. It does not work if they are deaf!

When I am walking, there is more danger from dogs objecting to a person walking on their territory than from anything else, especially if I am walking in a well-to-do area where people are scared about intrusions, so this little item gives me a feeling of security. Sometimes, there is the sneaky type of dog that lets you walk past, pretending it's looking the other way, then creeps up behind and nips the ankles. I can usually recognise that look in their eyes though and they are always cowards, frightened if I turn round and shout at them. Then, they will stroll off rapidly, looking round at the scenery and trying to pretend that they had no such wicked intention at all and had not just had to lose face and back off.

Anyway, I could see very quickly that this particular dog was no threat. She was very scared of me and any quick movement on my part had her bolting away fast. If I stood still, she circled around, creeping closer, really wanting to come near, but afraid. I kept still, not wanting to scare her.

A man came out of a drive, looking for the dog, because she should not have been out on the road and he had heard her barking. He took immediate pity on my wet, sad-looking state and invited me to come in for a cup of tea with him and his wife.

Trish and George was a lovely couple and treated me very kindly. Trish provided tea and cakes, taking my soaked map away to be dried on the Aga and hanging my raincoat up to dry as well. The dog too now accepted a cuddle without fear. George said she had always been that fearful, right from a puppy, without any known reason.

We sat in a lovely conservatory, looking out at a garden which they said lots of wildlife visited. We watched birds on the bird-table and a mouse kept nipping in and out at the base of it.

George did upholstery and I recognised the fabric I was sitting on as having come from a factory at which I had once worked as a temporary packer. I might even have packed it and sent it off to him. Trish belonged to Greenpeace and the WI and it was very interesting talking to them both. I noticed that they did not have a Scots lilt to their accents, but were definitely North Country and asked if they had moved up there. I was expecting the accent still to be Scots as it was so near the border, but

George said that there was a sharp cut-off between Scots
and North Country accents and not a gradual change.
There was a local Cumbrian accent, he said, which was
completely different again, but it was not heard very much
nowadays.

When I started off again with a nice dry raincoat
and map, the rain had eased off for a while, but it soon
started even more heavily and didn't stop again. I was
soon soaked right through my waterproof because only
deep sea diving equipment or a spacesuit would have kept
that rain out, but the warmth of all the kind people was in
me and I was not depressed. For the last four miles
though, I got sudden and vicious pains in my leg and it
became very swollen.

When I got to Brampton, I dripped into the
Information Centre and found that there were not many
places to stay within my budget. The ones that there were
needed more walking to get to them but, standing there,
just waiting for me, were two people who knew a lady who
was not on the Register but did B & B and she was just
down the road. Those people just happened to be there
when I needed help.

I knocked at the house I had been sent to, hoping
so much that there would be room for me. Another Jane
opened the door to see an object standing in front of her,
looking very much like a drowned rat, with water pouring
off and flooding her porch.

"I'm much more respectable on the inside than I
look on the outside," I said hopefully.

She laughed and took me and my sodden attachments in without a fuss. I enjoyed chatting with Jane over a cup of tea. We had quite a lot in common, including the fact that she was doing an Open University course. I had done this some years before.

Quite a lot in my rucksack was wet. Even though the future maps I needed had been protected by plastic, a pool had formed in the bottom of the bag and they had all become soaked. Jane dried them successfully on her 'Aga' and they were fine, but I found that half the route I'd marked in on each page had been washed off because it had been in felt pen. Oh well, at least they were unharmed other than that and I could soon mark out a route. After all the experience I'd had by now, perhaps the new route would be even better than the original.

How I longed to get a new rucksack cover. Either there had not been camping shops where I'd stopped, or it had been early closing day. Whatever day I arrived in a small town usually seemed to be the day for early closing. Different villages and towns have different days and I seemed to catch them with monotonous regularity.

I took painkillers and had a good sleep. The leg seemed a lot better in the morning, although still swollen. The forecast was rain, but it lied because it was beautiful all day.

At Castle Carrock, I asked in a shop if there were any tea rooms there, but there were not. Then a lady, who had been in the shop, ran to catch me up and took me home for tea.

Sheila and Dave were in the process of 'doing up' their house and a lovely job they were making of it too. I told them how I had found that people were so kind. I have had nothing but care and kindness all the way on my walk and it has been given to a scruffy nobody who must look less than respectable at times.

Now, on the walk, it was happening that I was coming across more pubs where I could sometimes stop for food. Today, I could also stop on the way to sit down because the weather was comfortable, so I rested more and it was good for my leg and my soul.

Much to my delight, on my travels, I came around a corner and surprised a man who had stopped his car and was doing a pee. He looked very confused and pretended he was looking at the view. It felt good being on the other side for a change.

I got as far as Lazenby. Tomorrow would only be a short walk to Penrith and I would have half a day to relax and sort out things before meeting Heather off the coach. I was looking forward to seeing her very much.

Today had been a good day altogether and it finished well too.

I asked at the Co-op if there was a B & B nearby and a lady just happened to be standing there who ran one. It was just around the corner in a lovely old house with more kind people.

* * *

30th May – A very happy day, because it was the one on which I was to meet my daughter. I had wanted to get there early and indeed, it was an easy walk into Penrith. I found a guest house straight away for both of us.

Penrith was ancient. Around 500 BC, it had been the site of Celtic occupation. The Romans built a road through it – I'll bet there were people darting out from between trees trying to stop them, but the Romans wouldn't have cared. Then Norsemen and Angles came to stay. It had suffered a lot from Scottish raids and a castle had been built as a defence against the Scots, but now, the castle was in ruins.

I checked out where Heather's bus would be coming in. Amazingly there was a bus station at one end of the town and a 'drop off' for coaches at the railway station which, naturally enough was right at the other end, as far away from the bus station as it could place itself.

I visited the bus station and it was absolutely deserted, like the Marie Celeste. Nobody at all was around and it looked as if it hadn't seen a bus in years. I walked to the railway station then and asked if the National Express stopped there. The railway man said, in a very huffy way, that they were rivals, so the coach certainly wouldn't be allowed to stop outside the station. He said that there was a parking space opposite, over the road, but denied all knowledge of ever having observed whether the National Express buses stopped there or not. So, I phoned the Coach Station at Victoria and they told me that, yes, it was opposite the railway station that the coach stopped.

After sorting that out, I was able to drift around

Penrith, which I liked very much. I bought another
rucksack cover, better than the last one and harder to blow
away. It would save me having to dry everything out so
often. The rucksack got noticeably heavier too, when it
was wet. I bought a new water bottle and felt that I was
fully equipped again.

Heather was arriving at about six in the evening. I
arrived early, in the unlikely case that the coach was early.
The ruins of Penrith Castle were right next to the stop and
I walked through these. I was surprised it was open to
everybody to walk through without charge. Somebody
else turned up to wait for the coach, so it really did seem to
be the right place, although I felt a bit anxious.

The coach was an hour late and I got a bit cold
waiting. Apparently, there had been a fire on the
motorway and the coach had to come a different way. It
was worth the wait though, to see the happy face of my
daughter grinning at me as she stepped off.

We hugged each other, delighted to be together.
She had made me a carrier for my water bottle, having
heard that my original one had broken. We went back to
the Guest House to dump her stuff and make ourselves a
cup of tea, then we went down the road for an Indian
meal. The people running the restaurant were short
staffed and it was about one and a half hours before we
got our meal. Some of the other customers were
absolutely furious, but we filled up the time easily enough
because we had lots to talk about. It was great to catch up
on news from home.

It was going to take two days walking to get to

Kirkby Stephen. There, I had arranged to meet a very good friend, who was coming over from East Yorkshire to spend a day with me. I was looking forward to that very much.

I had found that it was not easy to be able to say to people when I would be in a certain place at a certain time. Sometimes, when I had been walking, it was days before I was anywhere near where I could have met somebody off a train or bus so, with Helena and Heather I just had to estimate and hope.

Helena, my friend, had a car, which made it much easier to meet her, so we had settled on Kirkby Stephen as being an easy route from where she lived. When I could see how many days walking (hopefully), it would be before I got there, I phoned her and said what date that would be. Luckily she was flexible about time, which made it even easier because I had got to that area much earlier than I had originally thought I would.

It worked out that our meeting would clash with my daughter coming, but neither Heather nor Helena had minded that. So, I'd nosed out a B & B at Kirkby Stephen in advance and booked for the three of us.

Heather was keen to try the 'sleeping out' equipment that she had decided to take on her walk along the length of the Pyrenees. She was to start this walk when she returned home from the week with me, going alone and taking about two months to do it. It was a much more daring and demanding walk than mine, which was a civilised stroll in comparison.

We started off early the next day. It was strange walking with somebody and having to adjust my pace, but it was such fun having Heather there. She hated the idea of walking on roads, but as fortune would have it, quite a lot of the coming week's walk with her would be on footpaths. Her walking boots were not suitable for roads, which I had known would be the case and had warned her about, but she wanted to get her feet used to them.

We walked by road to Appleby. This place had had its troubles too from the wild Scots. It had been inhabited there for over 1000 years and had been transferred from Scotland to England in 1092 but then, those wild, wild Scots kept attacking it and it was flattened completely in 1388.

It was flourishing enough now though and full of tourists. There were caravans too, heading into Appleby from all directions. Many of these had already passed us on the road, beautifully decorated caravans, drawn by horses, with dark looking people guiding them. We found out that there was an annual gypsy horse fair held here and it was due to start the next week. Already the gypsies had started to arrive, some of them coming from all over Europe. It was certainly an unusual and colourful sight.

We walked through Appleby, even though I kept giving hopeful sideways glances at the B & Bs we passed. For once, there seemed to be plenty of those, when I wasn't allowed to have one, because Heather was very insistent that we would sleep outside that night to test her gear. I was happy enough about it really though, because it was going to be a fine night and the next night would be spent in comfort at Kirkby Stephen.

We took a footpath that disappeared into nowhere and were lost, so headed for woods down by the river. It had looked as though they were woods anyway, from a distance, but when we got there we found that it was only a line of trees by the river, so we walked quite a way through fields of grazing cows and some of barley. It was very beautiful and we saw hares and deer along the way.

We found some woods in the end and a nice sheltered place for our beds, so set up home. The mosquitoes and other biting things couldn't believe their luck at finding such a meal set out for them conveniently like that. We ended up covering ourselves all over with scarves, hats and any item of clothing we could and were in peals of laughter because we looked so funny to each other.

Then, we saw a man with a dog below us, so were quiet because, after all, we were on somebody's land. We hoped he'd pass by, but he didn't. It was all right though. The man was a farmer from nearby and, far from telling us off, stayed and talked with us for a while. As well as being a farmer, Geoff was a mountain climber and knew the Pyrenees well so Heather and he talked about them. He recorded bird numbers locally and told us a lot about the local birds. It was great talking to him. He was a gentle and interesting person and Heather said afterwards that what a pity he was married, she could just fancy a farmer like him!

Geoff said that he had heard us talking and laughing a long way off and had thought that we were gypsies. He told us that the town was thinking of stopping the horse fair because, when it was good weather, everything goes well, but when it is bad weather, the gypsies get very frustrated and there is trouble. Only from a minority of course, but it seems that it is always the minority that spoils everything for the majority.

Anyway, the previous year, the weather had been awful and there had been a lot of fighting and smashing up of property. Many local pubs would be boarding up their premises this year and so, despite the attraction to tourism, the damage caused made it dubious as to whether it was worth it, so this might be the last fair.

Geoff had not minded if it had been gypsies there on his land, he would not have told them to go, but he knew that they did hare coursing, which he hated because of the cruelty. They usually indulged in this early mornings so, if it had been gypsies, he would have let them know that he would be around and watchful.

I could understand the local worry at potential trouble but thought it a shame that such a colourful event as all those horse-drawn caravans might no longer happen.

It made a very interesting stay in the woods, talking to Geoff.

Heather had brought out more fuel blocks for me and a supply of tea, powdered milk and sugar. Also, she had brought porridge. She tutted at my lazy packet-coffee with milk. I told her how grateful I'd been to her for making me bring the little stove and how her briefing me on the dangers of hypothermia had enabled me to recognised the onset of it in Scotland. We cooked ourselves soup and noodles, with stinging nettles added.

My leg, although much improved, was still hurting a bit, so I was a bit restless. We were drifting off to sleep when, suddenly, there was a loud crashing, as some large animal charged down to the river, passing very close to us. The animal had pounded by just where we had considered putting our sleeping bags at first and would have landed on us, so we were very pleased we had changed our minds. We thought that it must have been a deer, but it sounded more like an elephant. We had both shot upright, startled.

When we woke in the morning, it was cold, but with a clear sky and the sun coming up. The trees peered at us through the mist, looking curious and mysterious. Heather did us porridge for breakfast, which was much more luxurious than I was used to when sleeping out. She had done all this in the Himalayas where she had not been anywhere near civilisation much of the time. On my walk, I was never that far from habitation. I could afford to eat sparsely from time to time, because I knew that it would not be long before I was able to get food, but she had not been in that position in Ladakh.

The porridge stuck to our ribs and warmed us. Geoff had given us instructions on how to find our way back to the route. We walked along a railway viaduct and soon found our way again.

It was a lovely day and, to me seemed an easy walk but Heather was not used to pounding along on tarmac. Today was all tarmac too and she had those walking boots, which do jar the poor legs on hard surfaces, so she got tired.

I was amazed that she considered I was going fast. I am not a fast walker but suppose I must have by now got into some sort of rhythm. Usually, she walked much faster than me and would have had to wait. I slowed myself down but found it very hard to do that because of the acquired rhythm I suppose. She nicknamed me 'The Road Runner' and, every time I forged ahead I heard a "beep beep" coming from behind me. Finally, we got a good system. Heather quite liked walking by herself sometimes and I like stopping sometimes and looking at the view so I would go at my own pace and then stop at a viewpoint and wait for her. It worked OK.

We laughed and squabbled. We always do that!

There was a funny time, when we were spending a week together once, walking in the Lake District and decided that we had had enough of each others' company for a while and would spend the morning doing our own thing. So we very amicably set off in our separate directions. I decided to go for a row on the lake and joined the queue for the boats, only to find Heather joining it too. We ignored each other and got into our respective boats. We both rowed out in opposite directions and then, when I was far out, I thought I'd just check on what Heather was doing, so I aimed my binoculars in her direction. As they focussed, I saw that she was sitting with her binoculars pointing in my direction, just checking on what I was doing.

We got out of our boats, glared at each other and walked off in opposite directions. I walked in a lovely wood and came across some rocks. I climbed them and sat in a secluded space among the rocks. I had sat there a while, when I heard someone below passing by, looked down and there was Heather, ending up at exactly the same place as me. I kept my head down though and only told her afterwards. That evening, we really laughed about it.

Anyway, now we were walking together again, getting on very well in our own family way and enjoying it. I told her how much I appreciated that she would understand what my walk had been like because others could imagine what it was like but not really know. She would experience some of how it was. It made me feel really good, that she had wanted to come and share part of it with me like that.

It was good weather and the farmers all along the way were silage making. When we got to Kirkby Stephen, we found where I'd booked us all in.

There had only been a single and double room left when I booked. I am very restless at night and so, now that I can choose, no way do I share a bed with anybody, unless there is absolutely no alternative such as both being exposed to lethal sub-zero temperatures and having to share bodily warmth and then it would have to be with that guy from X-Files. So Derek had kindly put a spare mattress down for us in the room. I was happy to use this, but Heather said she preferred to sleep on the floor anyway, so she took it.

She was tired and had a rest while I went out and, on her suggestion, brought some Arnica ointment to see if it would help my leg. It did seem to help.

When I got back I found that my friend Helena had arrived and gone off to look for me and Heather had gone out after that too, so I went to search for both of them.

Our world lines crossed at exactly the same place in town. It was lovely to see Helena again. We hadn't seen each other for some years, but now that we were together again, it was as if we had seen each other only the day before. We all went for a nice cup of tea and the two H's got along like a house on fire, finding they were both keen on diving. Heather had got herself a diving certificate in the Honduras and Helena had done diving in warm seas but also a lot in the much colder seas around Great Britain.

Crackers, I thought, both of them, especially in our own cold seas. Water is nasty, cold stuff and you can drown in it. As far as I'm concerned, the shorter time I spend in it, the happier I am. I get in and out of it for washing purposes as quick as I can, just in case my skin comes off.

Heather and I had the idea of booking into the Youth Hostel the next night, so that we could use the washing machine there. When we checked on it though, we found that they were shut on both Tuesday and Wednesday, so it knocked that idea on the head. So, we booked in for another night at the B & B because we liked it there very much. There was only a single room for the next night, but we could do the same with the mattress on the floor and Derek charged us less because of it. Indeed, the price difference between this luxurious stay and the

Youth Hostel was very small.

I'd been finding that, if you bought breakfast at them, some Youth Hostels had become almost as expensive as B & B's which was a shame really. I never got on very well with the sheet sleeping bag you had to use either, because somehow, I always got it all twisted up around me so that I couldn't get out. There was usually somebody with a loud snore in the room as well, sometimes even two or three. Altogether, I seldom got a good nights sleep and the price difference that had previously made the discomfort worth while was getting narrower each year.

Wednesday was a great day. Helena drove us up to beautiful moors in her car. It was a strange experience for me, being in a vehicle. She had heard that 'Gaping Gill' was open to the public that week. This is an underground cavern – a very large pothole. It's only open for a week once a year, when the local potholers organise it and when you can be let down on a winch.

It would be quite a walk there from our direction and I was a bit worried that Helena would find it too much, because she has ME and, when she overdoes things, suffers enormously the next day. She also has great courage and an adventurous spirit and says that she'd rather have the days of suffering than miss out on an adventure.

The walk to Gaping Gill was up and up. Heather went ahead but, when the way diverged had not reappeared and we didn't know which way she had gone. We asked somebody who was also on the way there which way it was and they directed us but, afterwards, we found it was the long way round and much harder. Helena managed fine, although I was concerned.

Being so 'up' the views were magnificent. We were confident that Heather would reappear, but she didn't, so I was a bit worried, but thought that someone who had found their way amongst the wild mountains of the Himalaya, would perhaps be able to cope with Yorkshire.

The way went on and on, over moor which was 1250 feet above sea level and we were not completely sure we were going the right way but then, saw some white blotches up ahead and it was tents. When we got there, we found the tents belonged to the local potholing club. They loaned us waterproof suits and hats, we paid our fee and off we went, each in turn, lowered down by the winch.

Gaping Gill is only forty feet in diameter at the top, which narrows, but then widens out funnel-like into the 'cave' which is 365 feet deep.

I sat in the winch chair, keeping my knees tucked in as instructed so that they would not smash on the rock and was lowered down and down into a long and dark hole.

When I got to the bottom, I was helped out into the cavern, which had been lit up by lamps. It was large, with a waterfall pouring down into it. It is said that this is the highest known underground waterfall in England. I looked up to the circle of light, which was soon blocked off by Helena coming down.

We walked around the cavern in awe. The sound of the falling water filled the space and it felt like we were on another world. Some proper potholers were off and away to crawl along tunnels leading from the other end of the cavern. I was sure that Helena would have been off with them if she'd had the chance.

The people who were in charge, told us that the stream had been diverted for the week. Usually, it poured down the hole we had been winched down. I didn't find that information very comforting. It seemed to me that, if a flash flood occurred further up, the stream could decide to reoccupy the hole. My interest and wonder in the beautiful cavern held off such worrying thoughts though and I was fascinated. Helena was just fearless anyway.

I had hoped that Heather would appear from above, having found us, but she didn't.

We were winched up again by a man wearing a jester's cap and walked back the way we had come, which was downhill and easier.

When we got back to the car, Heather was waiting. She had retraced her steps to try to find us and would have come on to Gaping Gill, except that a potholer man she met had told her in a snooty kind of way that she was not dressed suitably for going down so would not be allowed to and, if Helena and me had not been dressed correctly, we would not have been allowed down either. This, as we had proved, was absolute rubbish and showed that you should never, never, believe what so called 'experts' tell you, because quite often, they are talking through their arse – but with a posh accent.

I had learned from a very early age to distrust authority until it had proved worthy of my trust and, although the incident that led me to this opinion was a bad experience, in fact, it caused me to obtain freedom from a load that I noticed often weighed heavily on people. I was now able to ignore the fact that I was supposed to be in awe of a person because of their apparent exalted position in life. If such a person proved to me that they merited my respect through their behaviour and what they themselves were, well then they got it. If not, they didn't. Mere 'importance' of person no longer meant anything to me.

It was a great freedom and the early suffering in the obtaining of the realisation that led to that freedom for the rest of my life, might have been worth it.

I was very sorry that Heather had missed seeing Gaping Gill, but she said it was her own fault because she should not have gone so far ahead.

We all had fish and chips when we got back to Kirkby Stephen and then Helena had to leave for home, so we said our farewells, me intending to go and stay with her the next year for some walking around her beautiful part of the country at Thornton-le-Dale.

Heather had enjoyed Helena's company very much too. We went back and watched a James Bond film.

The next day was another interesting time. Heather and 'interesting' often seem to go together.

We started off on a right-of-way, across beautiful

country with hills to either side, over which hung black clouds, but where we walked, the weather stayed fine.

With nobody in sight, Heather squatted for essential purposes, when the inevitable young man appeared. I was pleased that it happened to her too.

Then, we spent a bit of time on a road and it rained. Gypsies were passing us all along the way, on the move. I hoped that the weather would improve for their horse fair.

We saw a railway bridge and trespassed to sit underneath for shelter and a hot drink. I peered up from under the bridge and met the surprised gaze of a couple who were photographing gypsy caravans. I waved cheerfully at them. When we walked past them later, I thought they looked a bit nervous of us. Surely we didn't look like undesirables?

Then, we had a lovely no-rain walk over the hills towards Garsdale Head. Heather wanted some practice with compass and map, so took them away from me. I immediately felt completely naked and vulnerable without them and followed her, bleating pathetically, but she just laughed at me and wouldn't let me have them back for a long while.

Take away my compass and map and a sense of panic comes over me. Armed with them both, I feel completely secure.

She gave them back into my shaking hands in the end and I felt a whole person once again.

As we neared the end of the day's walk and getting a bit tired, it was not at all clear which way to go. The path had long since petered out into what could have been paths but most likely were sheep tracks. We became lost and ended up walking through tussocks and boggy land.

We squabbled a bit over which direction to take. Heather said I was inclined to froth at the mouth when I got cross, which I'm sure is only slander. I wanted to go one way and Heather wanted to go ninety degrees the other way. In the end, we found we were both right. We went Heather's way and came across the little road we had been heading for. Had we gone my way, we would have gone in the wrong direction from what I had originally planned but would have cut across country direct to Garsdale Head. This would have saved about two miles of walking, but would have been done in complete ignorance and been totally accidental.

Heather's walking boots had come into their own across this sort of country, but my trainers were not good. On Heather's suggestion, I had worn plastic bags inside them to try and keep my feet dry, which worked, except when we had cut across the bog, when they got wet anyway.

We were aiming for Garsdale Head railway halt, hoping to find some shelter for the night. Both of us were very tired. I saw a phone box and phoned Steve and Suzanne, because they were back now from their holiday in Portugal. They had had a very good time, which they deserved and my grand person was still holding on in there, kicking away.

There were two waiting rooms at the station, but we opted for the smaller one, over the track, because we thought it was more likely that nobody would come in it. We cooked some soup and mine boiled over, at which point, two people walked in, looking for a timetable. Isn't that always the way? Usually, I am very neat and organised, but just when I'm in a real untidy mess, somebody arrives. I never leave any rubbish or mess where I've been, so cleaned it up straight away, but was cross at myself for having let it boil over.

There was a small stream nearby and Heather washed in it but, when I tried to, a host of tiny white flies descended, nibbling at every bit of exposed flesh they could find, so I soon beat a hasty retreat. The flies hadn't bothered Heather so, either they had just arrived, or I was a more tasty morsel. I expect they went for quality.

Heather slept on a bench and said that I should sleep on the other one, because it would be warmer than the stone floor. I didn't, thinking that it was too narrow and I might be in danger of rolling off, but afterwards, very much wished I had taken her advice because she was toasty warm and I was frozen.

I must have dropped off to sleep for a while but was awoken with a loud "Sssh!" I stayed still, thinking that Heather had heard somebody coming, but it was only to make me shift position. I had apparently been making little puffs with my mouth when breathing out. Maybe I was dreaming that I was a steam train. She had not meant to wake me permanently but I was wide awake by then, feeling huffy because I hadn't shushed at her when she was snoring a bit before that. I was so cold that I didn't sleep the rest of the night. I knew it would be warmer on the bench, but all our baggage was spread out on that and I couldn't be bothered to shift it all. That was probably extremely silly but, lying there very very cold in a railway waiting room in the dark, doesn't lead to clear thinking.

In the morning, we squabbled a bit because Heather said I had shuffled all night and it was my own fault I had been cold because I hadn't taken her advice, which was true and made me even more grumpy. The place itself was not at fault. It was dry and clean, with no graffiti and had been a hospitable gift to us.

The squabbling done and over with, Heather brought out the tea, milk powder and sugar (just for me, the sugar) and made us porridge too. She got the water, because she said it had been her job in the Himalayas to get water. I felt warmed from the love and care she was giving me, concerned about me having been cold.

It was really heavy rain, so we hung about inside the waiting room for an hour before leaving it at 7.30, when the rain had eased a bit.

The beautiful little road we now took went up a very steep hill for quite a long way at first. The rain started again, with enthusiasm. We intended to turn left on a footpath over the hills, but did not see a footpath marker anywhere, so must have passed it by. Maybe it was as well that we didn't cut off over those hills, because we were by now in low cloud and I don't think you could have seen very far ahead up there. Maybe my angel hid the footpath sign. Or maybe we had two angels now, one for Heather too. I hope they're the same sex, otherwise they might go off together, wings linked. Or again, maybe such a crude thing as attraction for the opposite sex doesn't come into the equation at a higher level of existence such as angel town. I wonder what the angels do in a power cut?

The rain was insistent and very heavy. Both of us now had plastic bags inside our shoes. We came to Lea Yeat.

Look," said Heather. "There's a sign saying 'Teas in Shed'

I gave her a very hard stare, because I thought she was just tormenting me, but it was true, there was a sign saying 'Teas in Shed' so, into the shed we went. If our angels hadn't led us past the footpath, we wouldn't have found that beautiful sign.

There were already four other walkers sitting there happily. They were walking the opposite way to us on the Dales Way. Because of the rain, they were making a slow start, hanging about in the hope that it would ease off a bit. They said that they had had very bad weather for the last two days, so we had been lucky because it had been quite good for us up until this lot.

One of these walkers gave me a really good tip. He wore glasses too and we both found that the rain drips off a waterproof hood straight down the lenses, which makes it very difficult to see. "Wear a peaked cap underneath the hood," he said, "And the rain will drip off the peak and not your glasses." I had a sun-hat with a brim all around, but Heather had a peaked cap that she handed over to me and I found it worked very well.

We had tea and a marvellous sandwich and Tony there talked to us and was very helpful, giving directions for walking part of the Dales Way, which meant we missed having to walk on a busier road and it cut a corner off our journey too. After that, it was to be tracks and part of the Pennine Way.

It was a bit muddy and slippery on the Way, but very beautiful, with stunning views of the edge of the Pennines. My trainers slipped quite a bit, but I was careful and it was well worth the trouble for the beauty around us.

The walkers had said it was to be rain all day and had reluctantly departed. It may well have been rain in the direction they walked, so different was the weather here from one place to another, but for our direction, the rain stopped and it was dry for the rest of the day.

After the Dales Way, we found the Pennine Way easily enough. Walking to it, we encountered some mountain bikers who had stopped at an intersection. I walked up and chatted happily to them. They saw the map I was using.

"Is that your map?" one of them said somewhat scornfully. "Huh! That's more like a road map. It's a wonder you can find your way at all."

Their tone was a bit condescending, as from the experienced and fit young to a geriatric shuffling unsteadily along.

"Where are you walking to?" another said.

"Horton," I replied.

"And where have you walked from?" he said, smiling kindly.

"John O' Groats," I said, "And the map has been OK, because I found my way this far.

Heather was watching them and said that their expressions were a picture, re-arranging themselves rapidly from scorn to a grudging respect. They were nice young men, just embedded in the assumption and surety of their youth that any poor old soul over 50 is physically incapable and a bit soft in the head to boot.

This attitude is often increased if the older person is a woman. Then, you also have to talk to them slowly and with a bit of a smirk to each other because, with an old mind that is feminine too, they may be finding it extra difficult to understand. If you have been female all your life and about half of the population is, you will have been used to this anyway, even before you are old.

Once, I was a member of an astronomy club. There were hardly any women in it and I undertook to make myself a telescope mirror. This was not unusual. Quite a few people did, because making your own telescope was so much cheaper than buying one.

After that, whenever I was introduced to a fella, it often went something like this.

"Let me introduce you to Pat. She's made her

own telescope mirror you know!"

"Oh! Have you?" the introduced man would say, leaning towards me and adopting a similar tone to that used in encouraging a clever child.

I never ever heard any of the many men who had also made a mirror being introduced as,

"Let me introduce you to Dave. He's made his own telescope mirror you know!"

"Oh! Have you? There's a clever little monkey then."

The sad thing was that the men didn't have any idea that they were doing this. They were being nice. They were being friendly.

Another time, I put up my hand after a talk and asked the lecturer a question. It was because I wanted to know the answer. Afterwards, he tried to arrange a personal and horizontal alignment with me. When I expressed my disinclination, he was very huffy.

"If a woman asks me a question," he said. "I assume she is interested in me," and he stalked off. I hadn't realised that lecturer was sometimes spelt lecherer.

Instances like that were almost everyday when I was younger, but my daughter says that things are very different now and I think she is right. Differences between the sexes there are and they should be rejoiced in but, to an alien, we would all appear as the same species!

We walked along the Pennine Way and came to a place where we could sit for a while by the river. It was very windy where we had first decided to sit so walked on around the corner and out of the wind.

As I got myself ready to sit down, I realised that there had been a big disaster! I had lost my map! I'd undone my hip belt to sit in the first chosen place, which would have caused the map to fall.

I rushed back in panic and hopeful pursuit to find the map but there was no sign of it. The wind had playfully taken it far away to rejoin my red hat. They were probably laughing together right now.

When I got back, Heather was laughing too. She said that, knowing how maniacal I am about having a map to constantly peer at, she thought that the loss of it would have unhinged my mind to the extent of running back miles after it.

I did feel very peeved, but when I got around to thinking about it without deep emotion, realised that I was relatively lucky. We were almost at the end of that page and the next overlapped it a bit so, during the next day, I would have the comforting security of the new page tucked in my belt.

It was reasonably easy to find the rest of the way to Horton. I had the route in my head, but at one place, there was once an intersection of paths where I wasn't sure which way was the correct one, so knocked at a farmhouse to check it out.

We thought that finding a B & B at Horton would be easy but no, they were all full. There was a Bunk House which was full too. We felt very despondent. We had found the last 5 miles a bit of a push – me on the rocks of the Pennine Way because it was hard on the soles of my feet in trainers and Heather had found the last few miles on the road hard in her walking boots.

Then, our angels stopped messing about with each other and came into action once again. Walking back to where there could have been a possible place of repose but with very little hope, Heather noticed a B & B sign hung outside a house. Now, that had certainly not been there when we had walked by not long before. When we knocked, the lady looked a bit surprised but said yes, there was room for us. She said she didn't usually leave the sign out and had only now put it there to show somebody who was coming where she was and was just about to take it in again. Five minutes later and that sign would not have been there and we would not have found her, but it had been there, just when we had needed it.

We were in a great old house, which had a lovely atmosphere, helped along by the lady who had welcomed us. After a good pub meal, we felt that life was absolutely perfect.

We learned that, although it seemed very quiet around there, the village certainly had its share of activity. There was a campsite opposite and the lady said that sometimes, it was very noisy. (We were lucky it was quiet the night we were there.) Once, when at 2pm, the whole lot were singing "Sweet Chariot" at the tops of their voices, she had phoned to ask that the noise should be stopped.

The farmer's wife had answered the phone and said that her husband could not go out because he was sleeping.

The lady had said, "I wish I could sleep," upon which the farmer's wife had replied "Oh well, its Sweet Chariot for you," and hung up.

That farmer and wife are at war with another farmer (and no doubt his wife). There have been occasions of punch-ups between them, to the delight of the local population. Life is one big sitcom really.

We knew we only had a short walk into Settle the next day, so allowed ourselves to sleep in later than usual. We had settled on Settle as the place from which Heather could get transport home, so this was to be our last day walking together. The week had seemed to go by very fast.

I had marked possible footpaths on the lost map, but we went into the local Information Centre and looked at their map. We saw the path we could take.

It was a pleasant way we walked then, all along the river, finishing with a little road into Settle, which we reached by two o'clock. Heather was going straight from there to stay with her Dad but, on enquiry, we found it wasn't that easy. To go by rail all the way was much too expensive and most of the coach times from Leeds were fully booked. It took a while to sort out, especially as the next day, which was Sunday, the first train to Leeds was not until 11am. In the end, we managed to book her a seat, catching the 11 o'clock train and then the 2.15 coach from Leeds.

After that, we could relax and look for a place to stay. That wasn't easy either. We tried some where either nobody answered the door or they were booked up but in the end managed to get the last places available at a Guest House in the centre of town.

So finally, we really could enjoy ourselves without any further worries and so walked for a while in a network of alleyways and small courts. These were lined with the houses they had always been lined with and overlooked by limestone cliffs. It was possible to forget all the cars and modern bustle and think that we had gone back in time to a more sedentary era, but then we came across a pub which made us pleased that we were modern ladies and were allowed inside a pub. As such, we could clutch a beer in our hot little hands and sit outside on a bench in the afternoon sunshine, smiling benignly at passers by. It was very mellow and gentle. We liked Settle very much, it felt unrushed and friendly.

Next morning, it was goodbye day to Heather. She walked a little way with me. I felt very empty and sad inside when I looked back and saw her walking away in the opposite direction. I hoped she would be safe and happy on her walk through the Pyrenees. She said that she had learned a lot from our walk on what to take and what not to take.

We had both really enjoyed our time together. Neither of us are lonely when we are by ourselves, indeed, we enjoy it, but being together is good too and there is always this internal wrench at the time of parting. I knew that, for a while, I would miss her.

* * *

I walked on to the next map. Oh joy! Security again. I noticed that there were lots of cyclists about.

At Wigglesworth, I called in to a pub for a very civilised morning coffee and there were two cyclists there. We got chatting. They were elderly, very fit and happy. It was interesting to hear that they both had very different types of bike in structure, but their speed and the distance achieved was about the same. They said that it depended on the rider rather than the bike. I thought that was very philosophical and supposed it was the same with life really.

I got to Gisburn and thought I'd stop there for the night. There was a large B & B, but nobody answered my hopeful knock. I hung around for a bit but realised that I could wait for a long time and then find they had no room anyway. I didn't want to risk that, so after a while, carried on.

I walked along a horribly busy main road with the intention of cutting through to a little road which ran parallel to it. I knew from the map that a few tracks joined that little road, but whenever I saw such a possible tract, it was not clear as to whether it was a route through to the road or just to houses and farms, so I kept missing them. It was a shame because it would have been good on the little road and it was horrid on this main road, with lots of traffic.

Again, the old story, that the names of the houses and farms were written on the map and, if they had consented to put their names up, I would have known if it was the track I wanted or not, but their names remained a well kept secret.

Along the way, there was a caravan site and I called in to see if there was any chance of hiring an empty caravan for the night. The young men in the office were friendly, but they were not able to do such an unusual thing. The caravans had to be leased for the week and anything else was not allowed.

It was cool, which was good for walking, but I kept having to stop all the time for every car that came towards me, because it was rather dangerous. Some drivers would acknowledge my carefulness with a finger or hand raised, some would smile, some would glare and others would look at me as if I had escaped from a zoo. A percentage of cars seemed to go by set rules which stated:-

1. Time your passing of the walker to when there is a deep puddle at the side of the road, which the walker has to step in, up to their ankles.

2. Alternatively, go fast through a deep puddle, so that you drench the walker.

3. If coming from behind another vehicle and the walker, overtake the vehicle in front, so that you suddenly whoosh by near the walker's left arm. That is a good one, because they most certainly will not be expecting you to be on their side of the road and coming fast from where they could not see you. They will now be sweating with fear, having jumped out of their skin as you passed and realising that, if they had wandered just slightly to their left at that time to avoid a puddle (because they could see the road in front was clear and might have just done that), why then, they would have been as flat as most of the local hedgehogs.

Just before Blacko, unexpectedly and pleasurably, I came upon a pub doing B & B. The people were friendly and I had a good meal. The pub was positioned high up on moorland and, from my window, I looked down a valley to what must have been Burnley, where the lights twinkled and sparkled as though they were alive.

I felt a bit 'down' in the morning. Thanks to the non-naming of residences, I had walked a few miles out of my way the day before and they had been unpleasant miles. Now, I found that I was one mile short of where I thought I was, so that would be one mile longer on what was going to be a long distance on that day anyway. One mile doesn't sound far to a car driver, but it is a long way at the end of a day's walking.

Also, it was raining heavily. And I was missing Heather.

I trudged grumpily along the hated main road for a while then – blessed relief – turned off to a small road.

Colne was a bit industrial looking, but I couldn't really tell, because I only walked through the outskirts. It was a very steep hill walking out of it, with a 20 per cent gradient, steeper still towards the top and the climb went on for a long, long way. The route I was to take was a bit muddly to find, but I knocked at a house and asked.

After that, I was walking in glorious isolation on a beautiful little road that was the old packhorse way across the moors. My bad mood started to lift again. I saw from the map that I was to be walking this road for 10 miles and that suited me fine. After the main road of the day before, the peace and fresh air were heavenly. The rain had stopped too. It was dull and cold but, no matter, it was dry.

I felt even better when I reached a reservoir and, standing by itself, was an old packhorse Inn, on the side of which was a sign that pointed up some steps and said 'Tea-rooms – Open!' It might just as well have been a sign that said 'Gate to Heaven – Do come in!'

I was by now used to coming across tea-rooms very occasionally, quickening my pace eagerly towards them, then being confronted by a sign saying 'closed' so couldn't really believe it until I actually walked through the door. It was 11.30 too, just the time for morning tea.

After lots and lots of tea and a disgustingly large slice of cake, I set off. There had been a lot of rain the day before and sometimes it was flooded a bit on the road, but I always got around the water all right. At one point, the Pennine Way crossed my route. It looked like it would have been pretty wet walking along that route at the moment.

These hills seemed even steeper than I had walked before, very tough, but giving the reward of the most beautiful panoramas spread out before me.

I had trudged a long way by the time I got to Heptonstall, but I felt fine. What a surprise it was to walk through Heptonstall. The village centre was shut off to traffic and had cobbled streets, old and unspoiled. The whole village was set on a moorland ridge and the houses had mostly been weavers' cottages in the past. At first, the weavers had worked in their homes but, when steam engines and thus machine driven mills came in, they had to go down to Hebden Bridge, to work in the factories there.

A pity that. It must have depersonalised the work and it didn't seem to be a very good change for the workers, only the ones who owned the factories.

Below me, was Hebden Bridge. I was standing way above the rooftops, looking down at it, with its terraces of many-storied houses all clustered together. Again, it was easy to imagine that I had been transported back in time.

Some of the countryside surrounding Hebden Bridge was nicknamed 'Little Switzerland'. Having seen the steep wooded hills on my way, I could understand why. The steep sided valleys cut into the limestone hills and were filled with a lush green and sometimes, there were plunging waterfalls.

My sister knew Hebden Bridge because, being in the business of machine knitting, she had obtained yarn from there.

A lady I met directed me to a short cut down into the town, which saved walking round the long hairpin bend by road. I walked down steep, rather slippery steps, then an equally steep cobbled path and over the old packhorse bridge. The way I walked would have, amazingly, been the main road once, busy with packhorses and people, all trying not to slip on the cobbles going down and puffing away on the way up.

At the Information Centre, they said that most of the accommodation there was already taken, it being a popular place and most people had pre-booked, but they found me a B & B not far away. It was a good one and the lady there did me a load of washing for £1, which was brilliant, because she had drying facilities too. Again, I put in my fleece and trousers. The only time I had worn the shorts was when I washed my trousers. It was a bit too cold to wear them otherwise, but they were worth carrying just for the purpose of trouser wash.

The next day, as I set off, it was with a feeling of apprehension that there was something difficult ahead and usually, when I get such a feeling, it proves to be well founded.

At first, I walked along the canal to avoid the busy road. The map showed clearly that there were lots of little roads and tracks but, when it came to reality, it didn't seem quite so easy to find the ones I wanted.

The good news was that it didn't rain all day, even though heavy showers had been forecast. From Hebden Bridge to Sowerby went OK, then I had to take a track through a wood, which was criss-crossed by all sorts of tracks. That is often a problem when walking in well used woods – there are so many tracks, it's hard to tell which is the one required. I went wrong, but not seriously enough to be the cause for my apprehension, which was still there. I'd had a nice chat with a lady who had put me right again and I'd only gone out of my way by a mile, soon getting back on the intended road again.

The hills were 'Last of the Summer Wine' hills.

You know, when you see Compo, Foggy and Clegg, on a hill, looking down at the village and, what you don't realise, but now I knew it, is that 'down' is vertical and they wouldn't have walked all the way up there – oh no, they'd have been dropped off at the top by the TV crew otherwise they might have had heart attacks. It was breathtakingly beautiful though, with views that couldn't possibly be real, but must be in a film and there were Norah Batty houses everywhere.

The way ahead of me looked easy enough on the map, but again, it was not as it looked. It was the same old problem that, If the farms and houses had put their pesky names up, it might have been easier, but again, as I had found before, the secret was well kept. Maybe it was part of a local religion that, if they let the name be known, disaster would follow. Bad luck for you if you were a new postman. So, amongst the myriad tracks that didn't seem to be on the map, I lost my way.

After a while, I ended up down the drive of a farm and asked a lady there where I was. I found out that I was not where I should have been, that was certain. She pointed to some houses way ahead, up on a ridge and said it was where I wanted to be but, if I took the road around, it would be a long way. She said I could take a short cut across the fields, direct to the road and save some mileage. The short cut looked like it was vertical down, then vertical up, but straightforward enough.

The first thing I found, after I'd climbed over the barbed wire, tearing my trousers a bit, was that it was welly-boot country, not intended for trainers. I sank in mud up to my ankles, but carried on down the hill, until I came to the stream which flowed enthusiastically at the bottom.

I imagine that this stream was usually a small one, easy enough to cross, but it had rained very heavily the previous night and, although not very wide, it was pretty deep now and rushing along at quite a speed. There were stones along the bottom and I thought I could cross by them if I didn't stop on any for very long, but I knew that I'd be a bit unsteady trying to balance with my rucksack attached.

It wasn't so far across. I could hurl the heavy bag over first. So I swung the rucksack a couple of times and heaved it over. It went across all right, but then, the silly thing rolled right down the bank again and into the stream.

Not wanting it to fill with water, I lunged out and fell in after it. There I sat in the stream, glaring at the offending object sitting there beside me.

"You silly fool," I said, "What did you want to do that for?"

It was then I realised that I had started talking to my rucksack.

I apologised to it for my harsh speech and we both got out. The rucksack hadn't come off too badly. The new waterproof cover had proved a winner and only the very bottom was wet.

The bottom half of me was very wet too, but I

knew the trousers would dry quickly. My trainers were, not surprisingly, swimmingly full of water, but at least the mud had all washed off.

I scrambled up the hill to the road, took off my shoes, tipped out the water with any fish that might have got trapped there, wrung out my socks and put them all back on, except for the fish. I wasn't going to risk using my dry socks and shoes, just in case.

I knew where I was by now and walked down to the Canal to Marsden, which was easy and beautiful walking.

As I got into the village, there were two B & B's in sight straight away and my hopes raised, but too prematurely because they were both full. People around were very friendly and helpful and told me where I could find three others, but there was no answer from any of them, so I didn't know if they were full or not.

I went to the Village Café and found that they were closing, but the nice people there said, not to worry, come in, and they told me of a Bunkhouse a mile up the road. That was good news. because it was on the way I should be walking the next day anyway.

I had been tired when arriving at the cafe, but tea, cake and kindliness had revived me. I thought it would be more likely there would be room at a Bunkhouse than if I waited for the B & B people to be back, so set off.

And a good choice it was too. All ended well. I knew it would, because the apprehension and foreboding of a difficult day ahead that I had felt at the start had washed off in the stream and, walking by the canal, I knew the difficult time had been dealt with and it would be all right now.

Forest Farm Bunk House was a B & B as well so, faced with the choice of a bit cheaper or really comfortable, there was no question about it as far as I could see after quite a tiring day and I chose comfortable.

Ted and May gave me and two other people who had arrived at the same time the warmest welcome anybody could possibly have. They brought us tea and sat chatting with us around a log fire. It was a very happy time in the beautiful old place that they had done up themselves. I felt very much at ease with these two lovely people.

The others I had arrived with, Pam and Les, had recently moved to an island off the North of Scotland. It was so interesting talking to them of their life up there. Les said that sometimes people moved to the island to escape something in their lives, but they usually brought what they were running away from with them, so it didn't work. He said, if a person was all right inside themselves, then anywhere was OK to be. I thought that was very wise and most probably true.

The rucksack soon dried out and so did my clothes after I'd washed them. I was a very happy bunny that night.

In the morning, at breakfast, Ted showed us his juke box, which brought back many memories from our youth. We chose our music. I picked some old memories and he chose May's favourite. It was such fun. I loved it.

* * *

My life seemed to be getting like an interference fringe with a band of light, a band of dark, then a band of light again and so on.

I waved goodbye to Ted, May, Pam and Les, who had definitely been a band of light, and walked on.

At one point, I had a choice of walking over more hills or going down into a town. Suddenly, I felt fed up with hills and views and fresh air. What I fancied, was a nice bit of pollution. So, down I went to Greenfield, which was neither green, nor a field. My body felt a bit tired and low in energy.

As I walked through a built-up zone, I felt better and completely relaxed. The pollution had obviously done the trick. After all, I lived near Gatwick and amongst traffic that sometimes reached gridlock. My body was probably so used to coping with kerosene and petrol fumes that it was suffering from withdrawal symptoms.

The information office was at the museum, where they were most helpful. There was a coffee morning there and a lady who was helping came and chatted to me.

She was surprised to hear that I was walking alone and asked if I was ever lonely. I told her no, not when I was actually alone and anyway, how could I be, when people like her were so friendly, talking with me the way she was.

It made me think though, as I have thought before, how strange it is that people, who share the same basic apparatus of body and brain, should experience things so differently. Something that frightened one person, like being in a dark forest, would be a pleasure to another. I like dark forests. They are beautiful and not scary at all, but the ones who are afraid do not see that beauty, just scary forest.

And, looking at the stars above them, one person would be frightened by the vastness of it all and not want to look at it, where another would find joy and comfort in seeing infinity spread out there and knowing that it was within them as well as without and there was nothing to be afraid of.

So – if I perceive that dark forest as beautiful and someone else perceives it as ugly, is it the same forest we are observing? If I were to look sideways quickly and catch a glimpse of what they were looking at, would I suddenly see a forest of blackness and foreboding? It goes the other way of course. If they looked at something they found beautiful they might not want to see it through my eyes!

The Information Office had told me that they had no B & B on their lists at Mottram, my next call, but there was one further on at Charlesworth. I tried to phone, to see if there was room there, but got no reply, so started off anyway.

I walked along the canal instead of the road and it was beautiful. Canals usually were. The weather was perfect. Now I had restocked with the pollution, I was ready for some fresh air again, so welcomed the little roads and tracks I now took. I passed through Carrbrook, which didn't take long and on to Walkerwood Reservoir. I sat with two lovely old men and a dog at the Reservoir for a while. They gave me directions in great detail of the way to Mottram by the footpath, which was the way I was going anyway, but I didn't like to interrupt them and reject their kindness.

As I walked, I had marvellous views over Manchester to my right. Nearer to me, there were built up areas in blotches, with some country in between. I wondered if the blotches would finally join up, squashing out the countryside.

On my left, the scenery was of wild hills. It amazed me, this sharp cut-off between the area of town and countryside. It sort of merged a bit in Sussex but here, where I was now walking - on my right was town, densely built-up and, on my left was country, sparsely populated. I was walking between the two.

At Mottram, a lady told me a short cut to Charlesworth that would save two miles. She said it was so clear, I couldn't miss it. Of course, I should have known better than to listen to anybody who finished with "You can't miss it!"

When I got to where I should turn off according to her directions, it wasn't at all clear to me. I'd phoned the B & B again, but still no answer. There didn't seem any immediate alternative though but to launch out and hope of a space there.

I got to a point where there were several different ways to choose from. I met a lady who was looking for a dog and asked. "Oh yes," she said. She knew the way I wanted and, with certainty and authority, directed me. Just to make sure, after I'd walked about a mile, I asked a young man I met if he knew the name of the farm I was headed for. He knew it, he said. It was just a bit further down the road.

I was pleased about that, because it was raining and cold. Much further than 'not far', I decided to check on my compass and found to my horror that I was now going North when, most certainly, I should have been going South. There was a house nearby and I knocked to try and find out where I was.

A lady called Julie opened the door. She hadn't heard of where I was headed at all, but looked at my dejected face and took me in straight away to give me a cup of tea and biscuits.

I could see that Julie had quite enough to do, with children to look after, one of whom was not well, yet she had found time to be kind to this complete stranger who had arrived out of nowhere. She said that her partner Pete was coming home soon and he might know where the place was. There was still no answer by phone.

It was all very frustrating. If I had not tried to organise ahead and been given the name of that B & B, I should have been prepared to sleep out. I could still do that and it looked as though I would have to. If I had not walked all the extra distance involved in going the wrong way, I should not have been so tired and, even if the B & B had been full, more willing to find shelter from the rain for the night. Now though, I was tired and cross at having been directed so far out of my way and lost when, if I had ignored all the advice and stuck to the road, I should have at least known where I was.

Pete came home and knew where I was headed. I could get there by a footpath, cutting across fields, but that was not at all clear, he said. It was a long way round by road but, not to worry, he would drive me there.

Even though he had just come home from work, he did this. And he did even more because, when we finally found the place, a young boy opened the door and said his parents were not there, but they were moving house and didn't do B & B any more.

Upon which, Pete drove me to another B & B he had seen. The lady who opened the door there looked at me and said "We're full" quite rudely, shutting the door immediately.

It was the first time anybody had been brusque like that but I think it was because I didn't have my rucksack on. I had left that in the car. My appearance was undoubtedly wind swept, I was tanned like a gypsy, wild haired and scruffy, but with a rucksack, all this would have been self-explanatory. I would have been judged as being one of those mad ramblers and probably quite harmless. That would have been acceptable but, without the rucksack, I had lost my identification. I was the same person, but judged completely differently.

That's a strange way to judge people isn't it – by the accessories their bodies cart around or by the clothes they hang on themselves? It is like you are stating what you are by all those things that you can put on and take off again. You could pretend to be anything you want that way couldn't you? People do.

Pete drove me even further, until we found a guest house at Marple Bridge.

On this walk, I was being constantly surprised and warmed by the downright kindness of people I met. Many people, hearing of what I planned to do, had shaken their heads sadly and warned of the bad and dangerous thing I was planning because there were so many evil and dangerous people around.   I had met none of the evil ones, only kind, lovely people. My tale of walking cannot be enlivened to please the eager ears of those who like to hear of untrustworthy and uncaring villains. There may well have been some of those about, but I had not met them. As far as I had experienced so far, Britain was populated by kind and caring people. What an unfashionable view!

The guest house was friendly. They laughed at my account of the last part of the day. It did sound funny when I told it in the comfort of a place to stay.

I could relax, at the end of what had been a bit of a difficult time and, listening to the cold wind and rain outside, mentally thanked Julie and Pete for the warm bed I had now found. I had taken their address so that I could write and tell them when I had completed the walk and also thank them again.

* * *

In the morning, I woke up at Marple Bridge. Now – there was somewhere I had formed no intention of ever visiting. Not that I had anything personal against the place. Until now, I had not even known it existed, it had not been on my route. Looking at the map though, I saw that I had only made a sideways leap. The walk to Hayfield would be the same distance as if I had been where I had originally planned so I would not be walking any less miles. I'd walked in silly circles enough the day before too, so didn't think it would be cheating to call it quits and take it from there.

On my way, I phoned Heather, who was off the next day on her trip to the Pyranees. I would not see her again until August. I hoped she would be happy and safe on her walk. My love for her floated over the miles between us to take lodging in her rucksack, so that it would be with her all the way.

Looking around, I could see why the Peak District was getting a bit overused, because there was all this mass of people living in towns surrounding it. I passed isolated houses and wondered about the lives of the people living there. They were most likely people who went into the built-up areas to work. It would be like living in a little island of house and garden, joined up to other people by use of a car. Not a community feeling I shouldn't think. The children would have to be ferried to and from school and friends. Often, it seemed, that appointments and arrangements had to be made for children to play with each other.

It has always been a wonder to me at how many

millions of different lifestyles there are in the world, all of them valid in the own way. People would be immersed within the confines of their particular lifestyle, with their own set of joys and problems. There were so many different ways of life to choose from. So, any way of life I chose, if not harmful to anybody else, would not be strange or bad but just one out of millions of different ways of living.

Thinking like that made it all right, just wanting to walk, however strange it might seem to others. I wished that I could do that for the rest of my life, as long as my kneecaps held out! All the minor difficulties during the walk had so far not dissuaded me that, most of the time, I was very happy and, at no time, had I even thought about wishing I hadn't been doing it.

With these thoughts and, happily grumpy, I made my way towards Hayfield. I walked about three miles, up, up and still more up. I began to feel a bit fed up with hills and longed to walk on flat, boring country for a while.

It seemed that I headed towards a crest of a hill, thinking "That's it," but when I got to the top, there was another crest in front of me, a long way off. There was always a reward for my efforts though, because, except in days of low fog and cloud, at the top was a most beautiful view.

This time, I got to the top of the hill to see Manchester stretched out way below me, as far as I could see. It was big. All those people. All those lives. All different. Most of them worried.

At Birch Vale, I found a small and heavenly café, with large pieces of wonderful cake and tea, so, after that, my spirits were back to normal again. I even chose to go on a little road marked with arrows on my map, which meant "Very steep and we're not joking," because it looked a nicer way.

The weather was good and – there were beautiful views!

Stopping at Chinley, I bought some fruit. I hadn't had fruit for a while and thought it would be better for my health if I did. I ate it sitting on a nice little village green. It was unusually comfortable, not too hot, not too cold, not windy, not raining, so I enjoyed just resting there for a while. In fact, that day, I was able to stop much more often, because of the comfortable temperature and dry ground, which was as I like it to be, enabling me to take the walking relaxed and easy.

I walked to Doveholes, where I'd hoped to find lodging. It had sounded a romantic, touristy sort of name – Doveholes. I was right inside the Peak District now, so thought I wouldn't have much trouble. Life is always interesting when you're walking though, because nothing is ever as expected. I might get tired, I might get wet, I might get grumpy and I might get puffed, but I never, never, get bored.

The landlady last night, hearing that I was headed for Doveholes, said that, in a car, you got through it so quickly, if you blinked, you had missed it.   With this comment in mind, I had eyed the fact that there was a railway station there somewhat hopefully, thinking it might

be a little isolated railway halt that had a waiting room –
waiting for me to spend the night there.

When I got to Doveholes, I found it was of some
size and the landlady must drive her car awfully fast to go
through it without noticing.

It was not a touristy place at all, I could see it was
a practical place, a working place. I liked the feel of it, but
it didn't seem to have anywhere to stay.

I called in at the Post Office to get more money
out and chatted to the friendly man there. He said he lived
near friends in Buxton, who did B & B and he'd ring for
me if I wanted, to see if there was room, which he did and
there was.

It was about three and a half miles further to
Buxton, along the main road. The road was much more
pleasant than I had anticipated it would be to walk along.
There was a cycle track all the way, it was flat walking and
with good views, so I trundled along with no problems.

I thought, as I walked, of the previous year, when
I had come up to the Peak District with a friend, walking
from Youth Hostel to Youth Hostel.

On that walk, we had passed by a circle of
standing stones, with another stone outside the circle. The
legend was, that these had been maidens, who had dared
to dance on the Sabbath day, so they, together with the
sinful fiddler, had been turned to stone. The stone outside
the dancing maidens was the 'fiddler', standing there so that
he would not get his toes trodden on I suppose.

Apparently, the legend had been formulated long after the stones had actually been placed there.

For no particular reason that I can remember, while standing by the 'Fiddler', I took out my compass and saw the needle move to the East, not by an enormous amount, but a definite swing. This intrigued me and I tried the compass on all the other stones, but it was only in one position, by the fiddler, that the compass swing happened.

Afterwards, I thought about this and it came to me that there could be an explanation. These stones had not seemed to be anywhere where you could see them for miles, indeed, they were in woods, so why had they been placed in that particular position? It could be that the woods had grown up around them since, but still, I wondered.

I reckoned that one explanation could be that a meteorite had fallen there, long ago. A brilliant ball of fire, streaking through the sky and lighting up the landscape, hurtling to the ground with an explosion that had been heard for many miles. After the fires had died down, the nervous locals would go to the place where the god had hurled his bolt, to find that the object had embedded itself deep into the ground.

Of course, the place would immediately become special and stones would be raised there to mark it.

If it had been an iron meteorite, there could be quite a large chunk down there still, which would swing a compass needle around.

Such memories and thoughts soon ate up the miles and I arrived in Buxton, finding the house easily enough.

It was a small, cosy house, feeling very homely and David and Tricia made me so welcome. When I left, I experienced yet another kindness when I was presented with a pack of sandwiches and goodies. For certain, they would be very much appreciated on the way!

After only a short while of walking, my route took me through a quarry. That is always a recipe for disaster, because quarries are so chewed up by lorries and the digging out of the land that there are tracks all over the place and sometimes the footpaths are not so clearly marked as they could be.

So it was, that I found it really hard to find the footpath I needed and, giving it up as a bad job, went by the compass in the direction I knew I should take.

At one point, there was a double row of barbed wire confronting me but the alternative was a difficult and long retracing over tussocky land which is always hard walking, so decided to go straight over the barbed wire as it wasn't all that high. I threw the rucksack over first, which muttered a bit at this throwing habit I had acquired of late, then I stood on tiptoe sideways and lifted one leg over, then the other. The first leg cleared the double strands of wire well, but trying to lift the second to match, my trousers caught and, there I was, with one leg either side of the wire, stuck fast. My rucksack sniggered.

No way could I release the barbed point from my

trousers, mainly because I couldn't move. There was only one solution. I had to get my legs out of the trousers. I did this, without any damage and ended up standing with a very sharp wind whistling up my knickers. Luckily, the visitors from Vega hadn't cottoned on to this interesting local happening and I was alone. I think I was alone anyway. You never can tell.

Released and free again, I walked on. The area of quarries was on my left now and something about it looked familiar. Then I realised that my friend and I had walked here the year before and we had got a bit mislaid around here then as well.

I felt hungry and stopped for a while, stuffing my face with the goodies David and Tricia had given me. Shortly after that, a sign announced 'Glutton' which I thought was getting a bit personal.

Looking at the sharp. pointed peaks of the hills I was walking amongst, I could see why the whole area was called the Peak District. It had been very steep hills but then, of a sudden it seemed, the countryside changed to rolling, easy, gradual hills. I was in Staffordshire.

I had been wearing my waterproof coat all day, but it hadn't rained. I got fed up with having to wear it because the temperature was too warm for that, so took it off. Sure enough, five minutes later, it started to rain, so I put it on again to make the rain stop, which of course it did.

Blasé as I had become to views, I must say I was very impressed when I walked along a ridge with a majestic panorama stretching out below me on my right hand side. I could see shining water and, from the map found that this was the Blackshawmoor Reservoirs and, rising up, was Stoney Cliffe which was, indeed, a cliff of majestic splendour.

I came across a pub called The Mermaid. How on earth had it got its name? How many mermaids did they get up here? If the pub had been open, I would have gone in and asked. It was cold up on the ridge, cold enough for snow and any mermaid venturing up here would get her little tail frozen off.

I came to a seat, looking out over the view and, despite the cold, wanted to stop and rest for a while. There was a car parked there but, as I got near the seat, the car erupted with a violent barking. The owners had left three dogs in the car who were now objecting to me sitting on the seat.

I was really fed up by that, not being allowed to sit in peace for a while, but I stubbornly ignored them. I couldn't stand the noise for very long though and had to go, but stopped and made faces at the dogs as I passed, whipping them up into a frenzy and hoping they would shit themselves in the excitement, which would just serve the car owners right for leaving the dogs there near a seat where they could pester other people.

I came down from the moorland ridge and the lower I got, the warmer it became. Soon, I was walking on flatter and mellow countryside, where I felt very much at home.

Leek was a very busy and trafficky place, with so many roads criss-crossing it. I dare say it had charm to be found if I'd stayed and looked around but, at first sight, I thought it looked a bit shabby. I got lodging at a Hotel. Although, as always, more expensive than a B & B, it was not nearly as good, being quite drab. There only seemed to be one very young person there in charge of it all and the large place felt empty and echoing. I don't think there were any other guests. It was the perfect background for one of those horror movies where there is one lonely guest . . . . .

I had a very small room, with a musty smelling shower crowded in one corner. The TV didn't work and the windows were frosted so I couldn't see out. I didn't like it much but at least it was a bed for the night.

The next day was of a perfect temperature for walking and didn't rain, but a migraine started. I had not had a migraine for quite a time, which was good. It was interesting that, during the past two days, I had felt a mild depression but, now that the migraine had started, the depression had gone away. I'd noticed in the past that, for a couple of days before a migraine, I had either felt depressed and very irritable or happy and excited in a manic and over-the-top type of way and full of restless energy. Anyway – whatever, here it was and I knew how to deal with it. I carried on walking.

I passed Foxfield Steam Railway, which was a small railway station, run by enthusiasts, I expect. Near my home, we have a famous one, the Bluebell Railway and I had in mind getting myself a day on the foot-plate of one of the trains. You can pay for a day doing that. I thought it might be a good way to celebrate my 60th birthday. It would usher in this new phase of my life and state the manner in which I intend to behave during what I hope will be an undignified old age.

I was heading towards Blythe Bridge, which I'd reach early in the afternoon. That was good, because then I could get to a chemist to buy some more of the tablets I used to help at night whenever I had a migraine. It was Saturday, so I didn't even think that there would be a problem with doing any shopping.

I got to Blythe Bridge all right and found a chemist easily enough, but the curse of the early closings which had chased me all along my walk, made their point – the chemist closed on Saturday afternoons. I could hardly believe that.

I walked on, passing a cricket match being played on a village green. That was not remarkable in itself, but it struck me as so English, so peaceful and pleasant, that I stopped for a while and watched.

It reminded me of those Saturdays with our Dad, as a child. Mum had a flower shop at the time so was not there on a Saturday so Dad was in charge. When I think of those times, I always remember them as being on a lazy summer day with the sound of cricket on the wireless. There was the calming drone of John Arlott, informing the country that a dog had just run across the pitch, that someone had a square leg, or had just bowled some poor maiden over. There was also a person who was a silly mid-on (or off). Alice in Wonderland was one of my favourite books and, these people playing cricket sounded like the games in that book, which fitted in quite acceptably with my view of the world.

The migraine was not such a bad one and I wasn't miserable, but it made me feel a bit weak. By the time I got to Stone, I had walked a long way and was very tired. I had thought that there would be no trouble getting accommodation at Stone. It was quite a large place.

I was beginning to get fed up with the constant hassle of finding somewhere to sleep, either an official place, where I paid for it, or sleeping out, which meant I had to look out for a good site and think 'food and water supply' too.

The walking part of the whole trip was easy enough. Those sponsored people, who had their accommodation all sorted out for them and didn't have to carry heavy rucksacks – that was not so hard. That just meant getting up every day and walking. Heaven! Still, if this was the way I had to do it, so be it. The alternative was not to do it and that was unthinkable. All grumbles apart, I was loving the experience.

But, here in Stone and still feeling a bit rough, I tried two B & Bs. One was full, the other, somebody had just beaten me to it and taken the last room. The only remaining place I could find out about was a Hotel in the Centre. That price was out of my willingness to pay. It probably wasn't expensive as Hotels go, but I didn't get that much income in a whole week. I didn't feel at home there either and should think that, certainly, they did not feel at home with me.

It looked like sleeping-out time, but I had an unhappy choice. It was getting late and had begun to rain. Either I had to walk out of the town for quite a long way and try to find a sheltered spot, or I stayed in town. I was happy enough sleeping out in the woods or country, but I felt very nervous in a town. With the migraine though, I really didn't feel very energetic or keen to walk much further.

I thought of Church porches, or a spare grave, but both churches were not that private sort of place, they were town churches, without suitable porches or land around them.

I had filled up my water bottle at a Public Convenience, where the tap had brought forth so powerful a gush that the water had run right up my sleeve, but now I had enough water to make myself a hot drink or two. I saw a dark tunnel ahead of me and headed towards it in case it was a good and sheltered place to stop. It was not very nice there though, damp and no good for sleeping in, but unexpectedly, as I came out by the river, there was an old and beautiful building that used to be a Mill. It had been converted now into the Mill Hotel and nobody I had asked about accommodation had mentioned that it was there. I was so lucky to have just stumbled upon it.

The people at the Hotel were very friendly. They were going through a bad patch because the access road to them was now blocked by a large building site for an enormous supermarket. It just looked derelict all around. Indeed, I had walked that way because it looked like I might find a deserted spot away from people. So, while this building work was going on, nobody knew the Hotel was there. The Council wouldn't let them put up a sign advertising their presence until the new road was built so, until then, their business suffered. I hoped they could hold on until then and that business would rocket up afterwards, because they gave me such a warm welcome and it felt genuine and not that it was just for my humble custom. The price was not as much as the other Hotel either, and very reasonable for a place like that.

* * *

Sunday was a lovely day, warm and sunny, with a breeze. The migraine had virtually gone and it had not been such a bad one. I was still free of the daily headaches, which was quite remarkable.

This was a mellow, mellow land and I loved it. The walk was on my very favourite little lanes and tracks, which were small and there were lots of them to choose from. The countryside around me was green and lush.

I was heading for a place that was right on the edge of my map page, The name of the place had been written on the next page and – that was the one that was still residing at home. When I showed people the map and asked them the name of this anonymous village, nobody seemed to know. That was puzzling, because it was very close by car and right on a canal, so I should have thought it would have been well known as a place to visit and walk along the canal. Maybe it wasn't really there, or appeared once every 100 years.

On the way to the mystery was a charming small village called Seighford. I sat by a ford and soaked my feet in the cool water. It was very peaceful there because the ford was too deep for cars to be able to pass through. As I sat there, I saw a movement out of the corner of my eye, looked up and saw a man walking along the roof of one of the houses. He didn't seem to be doing anything in particular, just walking along the ridge of the roof. When he got to the end, he turned and walked back. Maybe it was a local custom.

Just before Whitecross there was a family sitting by a lovely old steam engine. They looked such a pretty picture, all together in a group like that, so I asked them if they minded me taking a photo of them. They didn't mind at all.

At Church Eaton, I went into the churchyard. There were two cyclists there, Graham and Sheila. They lived locally and we chatted pleasantly together for quite a while. Graham mended a puncture while we were there. I was surprised at how quickly he could do it. I could quite see the attraction of cycling locally on this network of little roads that had hardly any cars.

Finally, I got to this mysterious place by the Canal. I had still not been able to find out its name, but when I got there, people did know where they lived and told me it was Wheaton Aston.

On the way to Wheaton Aston, I had begun to note sheltered places to where I could return, if necessary, if I could find nowhere to stay. I had eyed up a trailer in particular that looked comfortable, which was not covered but I didn't think it was going to rain that night.

I called in at a pub by the Canal in Wheaton Aston, had a coffee and some food and asked if they knew any B & Bs around there. Nobody did. I walked all the way through the village, but not a sign of accommodation anywhere. That seemed strange because it was a nice little village and situated right by the Canal.

Then, I saw a barn, full of straw. There was a lot of loose straw lying around amongst the bales too. It looked very comfortable.

There was a house nearby that looked as though the barn could be connected to it. I knocked on the door, to ask if they would mind me stopping the night. There was no reply.

I sat amongst the bales for a while, waiting for the people who lived in the house to return, but it was starting to get dark and still nobody was home. If I waited any longer, I would not be able to see clearly enough to arrange my bed in that barn, or to go on and find somewhere else if they said "no", so decided to trespass anyway.

I tucked myself away warmly amongst the straw, which was beautifully soft to sleep on and I heaped straw above me. It was the warmest I had yet been when in the sleeping bag and I would not hesitate to give the place 5 stars.

Some time in the night - it must have been late, because they were short nights and it was dark - I thought I heard people arriving home, but it was too late now to ask any permission, because I didn't want to hear them say "no".

Next morning, I was up, packed and away, before anyone else was stirring. Nobody would ever know I had been there. I was certainly not going to light a stove with all that straw about, so waited until I got along to a suitable spot before doing myself a hot drink and having some sort of breakfast.

Today was the day I was going to stay the night with my friend Helena's sister, Corinne. She and her family lived at Codsall. I had never met her before, but she had told Helena I was welcome to stay, so I had phoned a couple of days previously to check it was OK and say when I would arrive.

I had only a short walk to do that day because, on the way to Corinne's, there was Boscobel House. I particularly wanted to visit there because Mary, a friend of mine, had spent her childhood there. I knew it didn't open until 10.00 but had planned to get there thinking I would be leaving at B & B time and not at 'getting out of barn before discovered' time. However, because I was on the road so much earlier than I had expected, I now had about five hours in which to walk three miles. Even at my very worse, I was not that slow.

Fortunately, it was a beautiful and warm summer day, so I enjoyed the relaxation, walking slowly and stopping a great deal. I sat for a long while in a shady spot and read a book. I always try to get hold of very thin and light paperbacks for travelling. I tear the covers off and then the pages as I have read them, which makes them even lighter.

The time went surprisingly quickly and I got to Boscobel House with about an hour to wait, so sat there looking at the ducks on the pond. They sat and looked at me.

As soon as the house opened, I shuffled in. The man in charge looked surprised at such an early visitor on a Monday morning and not very thrilled about it. He probably liked to get himself sorted out before the visitors arrived. You couldn't go around the house without a guide, and the first 'showing' was not until 11.00, so I walked around the garden. I thought of Mary as a little girl in that garden. She had talked of it to me and now, here I was, seeing it for myself. I wished she could have been here too, sharing it with me.

Then, I walked into the field where the Royal Oak was standing, majestic and isolated. This was said to be the offspring of the oak that Charles II hid in when the Roundheads were looking for him. The original oak had been destroyed by souvenir hunters not long afterwards. It was funny to think that people were after souvenirs then too and just as destructive in the obtaining of them.

At the time of Charles, it had been thick forest all around there and the house had been surrounded by it. Now, not much remained, which was a bit sad. That oak tree would have been in very different surroundings at one time and seen a lot of changes. I wondered what it thought of these little bipeds scuttling over the field to stare at it, then scuttling back again. I wondered if it felt lonely now, all by itself in the middle of the field, with its mates long gone to that great oak forest in the sky.

Once, even longer ago than that, most of where I had walked would have been forest except for the very high places. There would not have been so many views, because it was all trees. You would have had to stand on very high ground to look over the tops of the trees and then, that was all you would have seen – trees. There would have been trees all over the world and, among the wild animals living in the forests of the planet, would have been apes. Some of these apes had come down from the trees and formed a breakaway group. They had learned a whole lot of new things. Some of the things were wonderful and good and some were not so good.

The ape's brain had become very clever, but I wondered how far it had really evolved, because the behaviour didn't always go with such a clever brain. Once, in London, I had travelled on a very new underground train. It came rushing into the station, shining and beautiful. If I had seen a picture of it when I was a child, I would have thought of it as being something from much further into the future yet, here it was, gliding to a stop, doors opening obediently. But, inside this beautiful train, the apes had spread their litter, just dropping it carelessly. They sat there sullenly, distrusting all around. There was no joy or laughter in their faces, no appreciation of the wonder of the train. Their thoughts were probably those of a complicated ape.

I had learned once that, inside all those heads, including my own, only a small part of the brain was actually working. There was plenty of brain left that didn't seem to be utilised. It was as if the rest slept, waiting. And I was asleep too, with all the others on the train. I so much wanted to wake up!

I woke up from these thoughts enough to go back to the house for the guided tour. Another two ladies had come in the meantime, which made it less embarrassing than if I had been the only one being guided. There was a school party being ushered around separately, so the house was alive again with the sound of young voices.

The tour was good. Mary had lived in the house

from 1932 until the 1960's. It must have been after her family left that the house lapsed into sad disrepair until English Heritage did a good job in renovating it and opening it up to the public. The man, who was the one I had met previously in the shop, was very pleasant now he had got going and made the tour very interesting, but I was surprised that he didn't seem at all interested that I knew someone who had lived in the house for over 30 years. Maybe he didn't believe me.

Anyway, I knew it was true and that the house would have been lively with children's' voices then too, because Mary was one of six children. She said that one of the rooms they lived in had now been demolished.

Mostly the information was about Charles and the time he hid. There was a hiding hole below the floor where he had stayed for many hours before taking to the tree. He would have been very scrunched up down there, because he had been a big man and it was a small hole. It didn't seem worth all the trouble really, being a King.

I liked the house very much and wondered where Mary and her brothers and sisters had slept.

I knew there was a tea-room at the house and had so much been looking forward to a cup of tea and something to eat after my sparse and boring breakfast. I found though that it was open six days a week and the only day it was not open was Monday. Quite naturally, it was Monday today.

I headed off for Codsall then, stopping for lunch at a pub on the way. A car pulled up alongside me.

"Hello. Are you Pat?" said a smiling face through the window.

It was Corinne. She had known I was calling in at Boscobel before coming to her and had driven around that way to see if she could pick me up.

"Want a lift, or walking?" she said.

I decided on the lift. It was a sideways jump again and anyway, so what? I probably would have found it hard to find my way to where they lived. I'm a specialist at getting lost in built-up areas.

Corinne was so warm and welcoming to me. Soon, I met Edward, who was four and Katie, two and a half. I had met them by letter from Helena right from Edward's birth and she had waxed lyrical about how beautiful they were. Now I met them for myself, I could see why she waxed because they were truly besottable children.

It was a lovely interlude staying with Corinne, Nigel and the children. Nigel is in the airforce. He had just come back from three weeks diving in Ascension Island, where he met a huge shark and tunas. It sounded an interesting life. The only drawback was that they never knew when they would have to move. They thought this might happen again very soon and they would have to go where the airforce decided that they should go. It was a strange thing that, with both families I had stayed with, the husbands were in the forces.

I looked at the map that evening and decided to

change my route from walking along a road to walking by the Canal. That was more to the East than I had planned and very near the edge of the map, but looked to be much more pleasant and the Canal was very close to where I was now.

Next morning, Corinne dropped me off at the Canal. She had done a load of washing for me, so I was particularly sweet smelling. I had really enjoyed myself and had felt very much at home with this lovely family. The smiling little faces of the children as they waved goodbye remained in my head for a long time.

The choice of canal path had been a good one. I love walking by canals and this was a particularly beautiful choice, the Shropshire Union Canal, which later merged with the Staffordshire and Worcester Canal. There seemed to be a network of them here, once serving industry, now mostly used by pleasure boats.

The canal wound about more than the road would have done but, who cared, it was easy walking, it was flat and no cars to have to keep stopping for. Occasionally a bike whispered by me, sometimes making me jump if they came from the back silently, but I didn't mind that because they always missed knocking me over and pleasant greetings were exchanged. It might be a good idea, though, if bicycle bells came back into fashion. I relaxed and enjoyed the wild flowers growing along the way. There were many water birds. I saw quite a few herons, standing like garden ornaments. I also saw several 2-spotted ladybirds. At home, I have only seen 7-spotted ones.

The Campion flower colours were so varied here, ranging from white, through all shades of pink to a very dark pink, almost red. At home, I have never seen a white variety, only pink. They usually have five petals, each petal having a partial division in the centre, but one I saw along the canal, had such a deep division that it had almost become a flower with ten petals. It was a particularly small variety too, but nestled happily enough amongst the others, seemingly unaware that it was different.

I phoned Helena on the way and told her she was right to be besotted with those children, also to thank her for the two large bars of chocolate she had left in Corinne's care, to give me.

It was a very good day. The holidaymakers in the narrow boats were so friendly. One boat drew in to the side as I walked and a lady on it handed me a Mars Bar ice cream. I was walking almost as fast as the boats. Often, I overtook the same boats again, while they were waiting at the locks, so people I chatted to seemed like old friends when I came up to them. It was so peaceful walking along and yet, not so many years ago, it would have been very noisy, with dozens of forges and steel mills along the canal. As I walked, with countryside spreading out on my right, I could hardly believe that, on my left, even though I was looking over countryside, just over the hill, Wolverhampton was spread-eagled. Again, there was this abrupt change between 'very built up' and 'very rural'.

I came off the canal to go into Kinver. "What a nice little village" I thought, as I walked up the main street.

Maybe it was the peaceful, happy day just walked

that coloured my feelings, but I believe it really is a nice little village.

My happiness was increased by finding a place to stay straight away from the information centre that was at the flower shop. I was greeted very enthusiastically by two beautiful eighteen-month old Labradors dogs, who knew straight away that I loved them. The owners were as welcoming but expressed it in a different manner than the dogs, which was just as well.

After I got settled, I walked back into Kinver to drift around. It was a long main street, winding around, lined mostly with red brick cottages. These were where the nail makers used to live, because the town was built up around the industry of wool at first, but later, iron screws and nails.

St.Peter's Church was set up high on a hill above the village. I wasn't around for long enough to explore all I would have liked. I knew of Kinver Edge, a sandstone bluff, in which is tunnelled a rock cottage known either as Nanny's Rock or Meg-a-Fox Hole. It has a flue running right up through the cliff and once, it is said, was a highwayman's hideout. You'd think that the Highwayman was caught and hanged at Hanging Hill, but that turned out to get its name because it was where the wool was hung up to dry.

I didn't find out until after I had left that the road up to the Church led past Holy Austin Rock, where local homeless people had carved cave dwellings in the sandstone. If I had known, I might have made the effort to climb the hill but then again, it had been a fair old walk that day, so maybe not. I knew that I should like to go back to Kinver in the future and explore all around.

That evening, I had a phone session to my loved ones. They were all fine and happy. Heather, of course I couldn't phone, her probably being on top of a mountain, but I thought of her and hoped she was happy too.

I set off next day into beautiful weather. The day before, I had felt certain that I would find accommodation and, so I did. Today, I felt that I wouldn't.

Worcester was too far for me to want to achieve and it didn't look hopeful for accommodation between Kinver and there without walking out of my way, so I was ready to have to sleep out.

I rejoined the canal at Wolverley. My legs had felt a bit tired from the start and my shoulders were sore, probably because the weather had turned quite hot which meant that I wasn't wearing as many clothes to buffer the abrasion of the rucksack straps. I had pads on my shoulders made of oblongs cut out from an old sleeping mat, but in hot weather, you sweat more and things rub.

For quite a long way along the canal, I noticed I was walking on stones, each of which gave the warning, "Danger, Cable 320,000 Volts Underneath'. That was nice.

Despite the tiredness and the sore shoulders, it was a very happy day. The fishing season had got underway and there were fisher-people everywhere, sitting on the banks. Just doing that really, sitting, for I never saw any of them catch a fish. I felt almost like an intruder as I passed, as if I should tiptoe by.

I had light-hearted chats with people. There were some people from Connecticut on a narrow boat. They kept overtaking me, then I would catch them up at the next lock, where there would be laughter and another chat.

Near Kidderminster, I sat down for a while. A lady sat too and got talking. She told me of the problems she had with her neighbours because of the parking of these neighbours' cars. Everywhere I went, people seemed to have problems like this, which seemed big enough when static, but not when you're moving like I was now. Listening to the troubles, it felt like they were coming from another world.

Talking again later to local people, I learned that people in Kidderminster were puzzled and distressed that the hospital was going to be shut and so they would have to go 15 miles to the nearest one. They said that nobody had wanted that and lots of money given by local people had gone into the hospital, so it was very strange it had happened and nobody had explained about the money. As we talked, others joined in the discussion. It sounded very sad and unnecessary that such a thing had been decided against what the people (who would after all, be the customers), wanted.

Shortly after Kidderminster, I came to Stourport-on-Severn. This was where the Canal ended in a big basin, but I found out I could continue walking South by taking the Severn Way and following the river.

Stourport grew up because of the canal system, but the canals didn't last in their usefulness for that long really, because the railway was built, which hasn't lasted in its usefulness for that long really, because the car has taken over and more roads have been built, which …(watch this space).

The first railway accident had happened at Stourport, when William Huskisson, a politician (so it served him right), was knocked down on the track and killed. There must be better ways of getting your name in the records.

The Severn Way had been a good discovery to keep me off the roads. It was a bit of a muddle to find the way to the start of the path, but a lady told me how to get there and then came and walked with me until she knew I was going to be all right. I appreciated that kindness, because I was sure I'd have been walking in silly circles otherwise.

It was harder walking along the river path than it had been by the canal so by the time I'd walked about 16 miles, I was looking out for somewhere to sleep. There were holiday homes with gardens by the river. Most were empty and some had porches, so I eyed these up as I passed in case I couldn't find anywhere else. A short while later though, I came to Holt Fleet and a camping site with a few caravans on it. Asking one of the caravan dwellers, it seemed that it would be perfectly in order for me to stay there. A lady came around every evening to collect the fee from new arrivals. It appealed to me to have washing facilities, so I had found my home for the night.

At first, I laid out my bivvy in a sheltered spot but soon realised that there were two things wrong with the place I had selected.

The first wrong thing was that cars parked nearby. I could see that, if someone came home late at night, especially if they had been to the pub, they wouldn't see me on the ground, flat and green as I was in the sleeping bag, and would probably park on me.

The second was that it soon became apparent that people cut through the hedge just at that spot to get to the site. I was sitting a short distance away and watched as people came through, stopped and stared at my bivvy, talking amongst themselves, then walking off, occasionally staring back at it.

I didn't fancy being stared at, or even prodded, when I was trying to get to sleep so picked up everything and transferred myself to a far corner, where people and cars would not go.

There was a small tent nearby, with two bikes outside. It was obviously a young couple inside who were engaged in a popular recreational activity, so I tactfully withdrew and sat some way off in the last of the sunshine. I watched the rabbits. If I didn't move, they came up very close to me. Later, when I rejoined my sleeping bag, the couple were outside, looking in amazement at the flat, long object that had settled down nearby and the long, thin one that now ambled up. They went off to the local pub and, soon after that, the lady collecting the money came around.

She smiled. "Is this your tent?" she enquired of me. I told her no, that it belonged to the young couple and this – what I was sitting on – was my sleeping arrangement.

"Well," she said. "It's £3 a night for a small tent, but I don't know what to charge for that. Oh, forget it!"

"I'm using your showers," I said.

"You're welcome," she said. "Good luck on your walk," and off she went, laughing.

I tucked myself in then and, early in the morning, long before the young couple or anybody else had surfaced, I was gone.

I walked over the iron bridge at Holt Fleet. This bridge had just one arch and had been built by Telford in 1828. Apparently, many locals choose to make a detour to cross by this bridge because the one at Worcester gets so congested with traffic.

The sky was a clear blue as I walked by the river. There had been no rain, but such a heavy dew and the grass where I was walking was so long, that soon my shoes became filled up with water. At one point there was a diversion to the main road. It looked as though the landowner had refused to let the path go through his land there.

When I got to the road, I sat down, wrung out my socks, tipped the water out of my shoes and put the dry spare pair of trainers on. There was a good path at the side of the road, so I thought I'd walk into Worcester and rejoin the river again there.

As I walked along towards a lay-by, a caravan tea-shop drove up. The man in it said that tea wouldn't be very long because the water was already hot. I said I wasn't in any hurry, so sat and talked with him.

His name was Michael. He had bought this outfit for his daughter, who usually ran it, but today she couldn't, so he was doing it. Then, he started frying up bacon for sandwiches. I come off the vegetarian diet for bacon sandwiches. The smell gets to me every time and I can't resist them. My breakfast that morning had been less than fulfilling and I longed for one of those sandwiches. Looking to see what change I had, I found I had enough for a cup of tea and a few pence more but then, only a £10 note. Michael didn't have much change yet, but he said not to worry, he'd do me a bacon sandwich anyway.

Talking to him, I soon realised that this kindness was part of his natural being. He was a very caring person and it was interesting talking with him. He had suffered from an accident at work and that had restricted him, but not in his efforts for others because I learned that he did a lot of work to help young drug addicts kick the habit. He felt very deeply about the problems of these young folk and wanted to help them if he could. He also helped to arrange walks for the disabled. At the moment, he was involved in helping to organise one where disabled people would be walking from Worcester to Cornwall and back. I could certainly appreciate the work that went into such an event.

As I was leaving, Michael gave me a baguette and can of apple juice for my journey. I just hadn't got adequate words to thank him for his care and kindness. People like Michael make you want to help too. I hope I shall always remember people I have met like him and be inspired.

* * *

I am ashamed to say that the only thing I knew about Worcester was that Worcester Sauce came from there right back early last century. The recipe is still a closely guarded secret.

The traffic in Worcester was terrible, with much more pollution than I fancied. Perhaps it was because I had arrived there during the morning rush hour. At one time, I felt a bit faint from the fumes, but then I joined the river again, which was better.

I looked down from a bridge. There was a squadron of swans floating majestically along. Sticking up amongst the beautiful creatures were supermarket trolleys, thrown there jokingly by the intelligent apes. The cathedral was an impressive sight as I passed it, showing that, when their minds were working differently, the apes could construct as well as destroy.

It was very lovely walking down there by the river but, as I moved out from the town into the countryside, the walking became quite difficult underfoot, with lots of stiles and rough ground. The grass here grew high and was wet, so I changed back into the already sopping trainers. There was no point in having two pairs of them soaking and uncomfortable.

Sometimes the path was right on the edge of a steep drop down to the river. Sometimes there were indentations, like holes and, as I looked down these to the water, sometimes, I saw the top of a fisherman's head. How on earth had those fishermen got down there – and how would they get up again? Also, there were places where the bank had been completely washed away. I knew that there had been floods in that area not so long before and I could see the signs of these in the fallen banks and detritus left behind.

There was a mass of the herb comfrey growing all along the way. The colours of the flowers ranged from white through purple to deep blue. I had never seen it in such abundance or colour variation before.

The fields I was walking through were long and narrow, mostly with grass as high as my waist, waiting for mowing. Some had already been mowed and haymaking was in progress. The contents of the fields were various. In some, I walked the whole length through nettles that reached above my head and cow parsley that grew even taller. One field was completely full of mayweed, which smelt delightful as I crushed it underfoot and brought back memories of my childhood. I also walked through fields of runner beans, peas, cabbages and cows. There was an enormous variety, never boring, but it did make for quite hard walking.

People on boats waved to me as they passed. Once, as I was resting, I heard haunting music approaching and saw that it was a man on a boat playing a flute.

I had almost reached to where I was aiming for, which was Upton-upon-Severn, when I came across a diversion because the bank had fallen away. The diversion sent me a long way in the wrong direction and finally, I came out on to a road. It was no good consulting my map because I had by now deviated so far across the page from my original intended route that I was on a page that was back at home. It was very hot now and I knew that I didn't want to walk all the way back to the river and then some more. I thought that the road was probably a short cut into Upton.

I asked a man who was in his garden how far I was from my destination. "Just down the road," said he. So on down the road I walked and on, and on, and on. By now, I had walked a good 20 miles, what with the wiggles and diversions and was feeling very overheated and tired. I was still in countryside, with no sign of a town or village.

Then, I saw a house. I wasn't sure by now if I was on the right road of if I was bypassing Upton, so I knocked on the door to ask where I was.

Another of my angels opened the door. A lady smiled at me, took me in and brought me tea and biscuits. She was interested in my walk. Ian Botham had walked down the road on his walk to Lands End she said. That was interesting. I was on a recognised route.

Upton was a mile down the road the lady said, but she would drive me there. I didn't want to put her to any trouble, but she said it was none at all and so I accepted. Time was trundling along and it was late afternoon now. I had walked so much extra through diversions that a lift would be no disgrace and I had had enough sun for the day. It really was so very kind of that lady. I was so tired at the time that I forgot to record either the name of the lady or house, which was a shame, but I hope she knew how much I appreciated her kindness.

Upton was a lovely large village. In 1651,

Cromwell sent his forces there. The defenders broke down the bridge but left a long plank, which Cromwell's men found was a pretty good fit across the broken arches and so used it to cross with. I bet they had a little laugh about that. The defenders would have been a bit miffed though.

"Who left that ****** plank there?!!!"

"Not me!"

"Not me!"

"Not me …."

I was in Worcestershire and, until fairly recent times, I would not have found it easy to walk in the meadows I had passed through because then, it was not meadows, it was covered with dense forests. Now, they have all gone.

I thought, with such a picturesque place, there would be plenty of B & Bs. It was not easy though. The Information Office gave me two addresses and let me leave my rucksack there while I checked them out. The first I tried was fully booked because of a forthcoming jazz festival. My heart went down. If there was this festival, then maybe the other would be booked too.

I found the second one. It didn't have a board outside and was tucked away so I should never have found it without advice. I was so lucky. A lodger who stayed weekdays had gone home a day earlier than usual, so there was a room free.

Gill made me very welcome. She said I could use the microwave and just make myself at home. It was sad. She and her husband had brought the home when he retired from farming, but then he had died, so it was not the sharing that had been planned. She liked meeting people and certainly it was a very comfortable and homely feeling there.

I collected my rucksack. It was Thursday and, surprise surprise, that was early closing day in Upton, but food shops were open.

Gill had friends coming that evening. It was a group who met once a month and tonight, a conservation lady was coming to take them on a guided walk around water meadows at the back of the house. Gill said I'd be very welcome to join them, so I did.

What a lovely bunch of ladies they all turned out to be. Even though I was amongst strangers, it didn't feel like that at all, because they were so friendly and made me feel so welcome and included.

The information on the water meadows was fascinating. They are very rare now and Worcestershire has the most. I had unknowingly been walking through them all along the river. The farming on them is strictly controlled to conserve the meadows. Hay is only allowed to be cut after the grasses have seeded and cattle are taken off the land during winter. The lady talking to us pointed out the typical vegetation of the meadows. There were so many plants, grasses and flowers, some of which I had not seen before.

There was a beautiful sky above as we walked, with mares-tail clouds and suddenly, looking in the direction of the sun, I saw sun-dogs. I had seen one before, but it was the first time I had seen the pair.

Sun-dogs (parahelia) are patches of shimmering light, one each side of the sun. They are refracted images of the sun, caused by hazy clouds of ice crystals in the atmosphere. These crystal clouds are not very thick and, as the sunlight passes through them, the crystals act like myriads of tiny prisms. Usually, the phenomenon appears as a halo, but sometimes as patches.

One of the 'dogs' we were looking at here was of rainbow colours, the other was like a small sun. That thrilled me, seeing them and I was pleased that I had been able to share something that I knew about with my new friends.

The Malverns were on our left. The sun was setting behind them, making them look like volcanoes. They are inliers made of old, old volcanic rock. It is Pre-Cambrian and some of the oldest, hardest rock on this planet. When the rock had risen and stuck up from the primeval sea there was what was to become Worcestershire but admittedly in a different shape then. Later, the sea shrank to shallow lakes and forests came and went. Not the forests we would know, but the giant hollow fern-trees with spores rather than seeds. You wouldn't have recognised the place. Then the forests got all squashed into coal, the lakes dried out and left salt deposits, sand and mud. Then, it all went down again, sea was above and limestone formed below, ice ages came and went, boulders were swept down from Scotland, the river altered course and – Worcestershire began to look familiar. Special, pure water is obtained from the Malverns and bottled. It gushes out where the porous rock meets the impervious.

It was altogether a wonderful evening, spent with lovely people.

Next morning, breakfast had been laid out for me in the visitor's room, but we both decided to ignore that and I had breakfast in the kitchen with Gill, which was much nicer. She had made my stay such a memorable time.

* * *

It was going to be a hot day. Getting out of the village to the road I needed was a bit confusing. A man directed me with great confidence but, after a while, my compass said I was going the wrong way. I retraced my steps and got myself pointed in the right direction.

I decided to walk on the road because the river way was much longer and I fancied a shorter day, but at first the roads were quite busy because there was a big show on that day. It eased though and I cut off on little roads.

At Long Green, I saw a pub with a sign stating what was on offer. It included coffee and also said "Friendly People". It was 11.30, so I welcomed the chance of a cup of coffee.

I stepped inside. It was spacious and empty. I was the only customer, but I went over to a corner so that I could tuck my rucksack out of anybody's way, as I always do.

"Would you mind taking your rucksack outside," said a loud and harsh voice. It was a command, certainly not a request.

Surprised, I took the offending item out into the hall, to where I could still see it.

"Can I put it here in this corner?" I said, very politely. "I don't like it being out of sight."

"I can't have it in here!" was the decision and the landlord stalked off.

Now, a landlord can choose who or what to have in his pub and I can choose whether to be there or not, so I removed my offensive rucksack and myself. I left quietly and without comment, which was a measure of how mellow and peaceful I had become on this walk. He didn't know how lucky he was.

I should not like to be slanderous and name the pub, but it had obviously been named in relation to the days when people hunted nearby. I did think that the sign stating the friendliness of the people was rather against the Trade Description Act. In fairness, I must state that it has probably now changed ownership. No wonder it had been empty.

In the whole time I had been away, that was the first time I had received that sort of welcome in a pub or anywhere else. It wasn't so bad. I had rather fancied a cup of coffee but I wasn't going to give that man my most valuable custom, so went down the road and drank water instead, which was probably much healthier and certainly cheaper.

I hoped though that the attitude wasn't going to be typical of the more affluent south, which I was now walking into, where appearance often counts for so much. I was a little bit short on appearance.

It was very hot by now so, even though the way was pleasant, I was getting tired. I followed a track, which disappeared towards the end, as is often the habit with tracks, so ended up cutting across 'set aside' land with weeds up to my nose and almost falling down a vertical slope.

I came out onto a main road, right where there was a garage with a shop. That was a lifesaver and, after an ice-cream and a drink, I felt renewed in energy as I headed towards Gloucester. There was a nice little road to walk on for most of the way.

It was a bit of an industrial route that I took into Gloucester and it was the biggest town I had settled in for some time, I liked the feel of the place. It goes back a long way does Roman Glevum, but the Romans wouldn't recognise the place now. I came into it near the docks, which was good because I planned to join the Gloucester and Sharpness Canal the next day.

I definitely felt a bit off-colour by the time I arrived. I hadn't got acclimatised to the heat yet and the small of my back was rubbed raw from sweating and the abrasion of the rucksack so I settled at the first place I could find, which was a Greek café that did accommodation as well. It was OK and the owner was friendly enough but I had to pay in advance. Maybe he'd had some bad experience, but I don't know how fast he thought I could run with my rucksack. Or maybe I was beginning to look like a tramp. Surely not.

After I'd rested a bit, I went up the road to the shopping centre, which was deserted now, but MacDonalds was open. Marvellous. I took away a vegeburger, chips and ice-cream and sat on a seat in the square to eat them, all mixed up as I fancied. Chips and ice-cream go very well together.

I felt better after that, though had a slight headache. As sat in my room, I could hear seagulls. It was a lovely, melancholy sound, speaking to me of travel and mysterious places. The setting sun was red and I wondered what it would be like to live on a planet with a red sun in the sky. I had this feeling that the sky would look yellow, but don't know why. It didn't seem too strange a thought. A red sun and yellow sky wouldn't be so bad, just different.

The next day was Saturday, 19th June. My body and mind felt very 'down'. I wasn't sure why, except that I still felt a bit under the weather. I decided on trying for a short day's walking and being able to stay somewhere inside that night, so looked at the map. If I diverted my plan of route just a bit, I could get to Stonehouse. I had been reassured from chatting to people that there would be plenty of B & B's at Stonehouse.

Knowing that the walk would not be so long, I took the more lengthy but much more pleasant route along the Canal and then down little roads.

I had a bit of a false start when an elderly gentleman on a bike cautioned me to walk down the left side of the Canal, because he said you couldn't get through after a while if you took the other side. As I reached the start, he came cycling up to catch me and said he had been wrong, it was the right side I should walk. Unfortunately, he had been correct the first time. I walked quite a way until I found I had to come back and start again. He was such a nice man and meant well. I'm sure he would have been very distressed to know he had sent me on the wrong way after all.

This Canal was very different from the previous

one. It was much wider, pleasant enough, but not so easy-going or personal.

After the false start, it was a pretty uneventful day, with nothing bad happening, but I still felt 'down' when I got to Stonehouse. I looked and again, I looked, but could not see any of those numerous B & B's that I had been assured of. I went into a charity shop to ask. The ladies there were very kind. They didn't know of any place in Stonehouse but looked up in the telephone book and found two farms that did accommodation. Each were more than a mile away, in opposing directions. They let me phone. It was easy for me to use phones because I had my own codes which sent the charge right through to my bank account, but I'm sure the ladies were not worrying about that because they were so pleasant and helpful.

Both the farms were full though, so it was the same old hassle that I was getting fed up with every evening, more so that day because I was not feeling much like dealing with hassle. 98% of the time, I was only too pleased to be organising myself, but that day, I was in the 2% band when I should have really welcomed a support vehicle to come trundling up and transport me to food and comfort.

The ladies told me that buses passed by regularly just over the road and went to Stroud, which was not far away. They suggested that I went there. If I had been feeling my normal self, I should have shuffled off and found a barn, woods, field or something, but the 'knowing' part of me was telling me not to be daft. Today was a time I was 'under the weather' and had to take care.

So I listened to what I knew and took the bus. It was a sideways jump again and I would end up walking more miles anyway, so that was all right.

I liked Stroud, I really did. It had a good feel. Apparently, it's not such a popular place for tourists, but I don't know why. It was one of those towns that, when someone should say, "Out of the towns you've gone so quickly through, are there any you would choose to live in," I should include Stroud, but without any logic, just how I felt.

I called at the Information Centre and booked a B & B that was on the outskirts of Stroud in the direction I was going to take the next day. Then I found an eating place called 'Mother Nature, where I ate the best food I had had for a long time and took some away with me for later.

When I'm walking, I don't feel hungry. I could easily not eat at all, but make myself have something, whether I feel hungry or not. It would be easy not to bother, but that would be really stupid. I wouldn't expect a car to run very well without putting petrol in it and food is my body's petrol. It doesn't worry me much though what I eat. I try and make it healthy, but often its junk food.

I had really enjoyed that food and was already beginning to feel better which was improved still further by arriving at the B & B, where Anne and John made me most welcome. On the way there, I had encountered another helpful coincidence. I wasn't quite sure I was going in the right direction and had asked a lady passing, but without much hope that she knew of 'Glenlyn'. "Oh yes," she said. "A friend of mine, coming up for a wedding, is staying there tomorrow."

The room I was in was an attic one. I love those, I feel so cosy in them. On the bed, was the most beautifully embroidered bedspread. Anne said she had put it on when she heard that it was a lady coming and that made me feel very cared for.

I was definitely on the mend from the bad patch. This rest and comfort was just what I had needed. I watched Sean Connery on the Box as James Bond and that completed the cure.

The next morning, I felt good again. I was heading towards Bath, to stay the night with my friend Gladys, aiming to get there on Tuesday. I had recovered completely from whatever it was that I'd had and the day was sunny, with scudding clouds and cool. There had been rain overnight, so the countryside had the clean smells you get after such rain.

Wild roses were growing along the way and the whiff of scent from them as I passed was delightful. Once, I stopped to smell one and vacuumed an insect up my left nostril. After a while, I managed to snort the poor creature out again but, regrettably, it was the worse for its experience and I had obviously ruined its day.

The 'B' road was very busy. I couldn't work out why there was so much traffic. After all, it was Sunday morning. All these drivers should have been in bed, enjoying a cup of tea and reading the Sunday newspapers.

What were they all doing out here on the road and driving like maniacs? I couldn't think that there were so many people late for Church.

They seemed to be going extra mad that morning. Cars would come rushing around the bends, careless of what might be there round the blind corners. I could hear them coming and had already flattened myself into the hedge, but don't know what chance a cyclist would have stood. It was another sign I was in the South now. Everybody seemed to be in a hurry.

I escaped to a small road and the lovely village of Nympsfield. Ancient sites were all around me. There was Nympsfield Long Barrow, Hatty Peglar's Tump and Uley Bury Fort, all close to each other, so the land had seen people with packs on their backs for a long time and the old trees I passed by took it as normal.

At Nympsfield, the pub said 'Open all Day' but the people looked surprised when I walked in. They soon recovered though and made me welcome with a nice cup of coffee. There was a phone box nearby and, it being Sunday morning, I phoned a few friends to let them know I was alive. My friend Joyce was planning to come out with me for a week on 26th June. I wasn't quite sure where I'd be to meet her yet. It had to be somewhere where there was a railway station. I thought it likely that I should have reached Taunton by then.

I had solved the problem of my back being rubbed raw in the heat by taking the bit of foam I used as a pillow when sleeping out and stuffing it between the rucksack and my back. Foam is one of the modern essentials for my travelling. It weighs almost nothing and eases a lot of places on the body.

I arrived, quite early on that pleasant afternoon, at Wotton-under-Edge. As I walked into the village, I passed the Ram Inn. It wasn't actually an Inn now, just a house. It was a beautiful old building and had newspaper cuttings stuck inside somewhat grubby windows, giving details of how haunted it was. The cuttings stated that it was reputedly the most haunted house in Britain. A staircase had once been dug out and a ghost baby had been heard crying. People had refused to stay in certain rooms. There was a notice that said 'Open Day'. I was interested in seeing inside, but nobody was around.

It is a strange thing about ghosts as to whether they are fact or not. I have an open mind on the subject.

Once, I was walking through a graveyard at around midnight, on the way home from a friend's. I had not thought for one moment that there would be anything frightening there and nor there was. I sat for a while inside a huge yew tree that had been there long before the birth of Christ, when Sussex had been covered with forest. It had felt good sitting inside that ancient tree and no thought of strange and creepy things entered my mind. It's odd anyway that people expect 'ghosts' to hang around graveyards. I can't think why. If I was a ghost, I could think of much better places to be.

Anyway, after leaving the graveyard, I had walked on and passed the old house, which was empty at the time, in between owners. The house was floodlit, so not even mysteriously dark and what happened next was not from an imagination that expected anything strange.

I was passing the house when the hairs on the back of my neck stood up and I knew that somebody was watching me. I was not in danger, but I was unwelcome. There was somebody watching who didn't want me there.

I became quite happy not to be there and walked more rapidly to please them. As soon as I got through the gates, the feeling went and the hairs subsided peacefully. I cut off through dark and cosy woods and it felt safe and OK. Later, I found out that an old lady had used to own the house and she did not like people much. There was the footpath passing the house so she could not alter the fact of people walking by but, when she was alive, she used to sit and glare at them from the windows. Still does, I reckon. More pity for her, wasting her time glaring at earthlings when she could be wandering about the galaxy.

Anyway, no hairs stood to attention while passing the Ram and I walked down into Wotton.

Straight away, I found a Guesthouse in the main street. It was early, only 3.00, but I settled in and it left me with the rest of the day to relax. It had been so easy that day and I was enjoying it.

The Town Hall was serving tea and cakes, so I wandered in and soon got chatting with a very friendly mother and daughter, who told me interesting things.

The Ram Inn was apparently owned by a strange man, who didn't let the locals in to look at his place, only tourists. It was thanks to him though that the house is still there, because even though rumoured that it could be the oldest house in England, there were plans to demolish it at one time for road widening. It seemed amazing to me that the old house had almost been knocked down but this man bought it and put in a lot of work and money to bring it back from a state of dereliction.

He's upset a few people though, especially the archaeologists. There were stone sarcophaguses found with daggers inside them, but he scrubbed the insides with wire wool to make them clean. That really miffed the experts, who wanted to see if there were DNA samples left inside but now would only get wire wool. So they won't let him have a grant for any more work.

I reckon he's entitled to be a bit eccentric though. He did save the dear old house and will no doubt haunt it in his turn. The daughter said she didn't know about ghosts, but when she was small, the kids would creep up at night and tap on the windows. And they probably still do. There is reputed to be a passage leading from the house to Market Street, made in Cromwell's time, so that the Bishop could escape.

Wotton was completely burned down in King John's reign.

"OK. Stand up the one who left the chip pan on!"

The main street is all back to front. Originally, the street was just an alleyway at the backs of the houses, but at some time it was all reversed, so it is the backs of the buildings that now line the main street. The fronts all point the other way and the building I was staying in was most beautiful in structure and impressive from the back – but then, the back was the front really!

When I returned to my pleasant lodgings, I sat for a while in the walled garden, enjoying the last of the sunshine. The view from my room was down into the garden and across it to a castle-like tower, on top of which was a sculpture of what looked like a pregnant dog, staring up into the sky.

I went to bed feeling well and happy.

During the night, I awoke and felt uneasiness. I sat up and put the bedside light on and then, froze in horror! I had seen a movement and there, plodding slowly across the snow-white duvet, was a black, black spider. This was no ordinary spider. This was the Arnold Schwarzeneggar of spiders. It was huge with thick limbs, built like a small (but not that small) tarantula. For a person who was scared of less well endowed spiders, this was a nightmare.

I jerked the duvet onto the floor and the spider plodded on. It didn't rush, just plodded steadfastly in a straight line. Now what to do? There was no way could I share the room with it.

I summoned up all my courage and got the toothbrush glass, which I placed sideways, in front of the spider. It shuffled on, straight into the glass. Then, I did a brave and terrible thing. I carried the glass, which was half full of spider, to the window and tipped it out.

I sat on the bed shaking and thought about it.

At first, I was proud of myself for overcoming my fear, but as I thought, I became more and more ashamed and regretful.

That spider now. At no time had it moved fast. It had merely plodded along. That must have meant it was a very old spider. Its huge size would also lead to that conclusion. And it had walked straight into the glass. Spiders don't usually walk willingly into a trap like that. They dodge around a bit, but this one had merely plodded steadfastly on. Was it blind as well?

So, what had I done? I had set about an old and, possibly blind, spider, who had probably lived in this room all its life. It was its home and it had every right to be there. I was a fleeting visitor, with no rights at all and I had thrown this poor innocent spider together with its rights, out of the window.

I hoped it had floated down to earth gently and found a way back in but, remembering its thick heavy body, it more likely went 'whizz' 'plop!' and I had probably caused it great harm.

I felt really bad about it. What I should have done was to take it out of the room, up the hall and let it loose where it could be cosy, warm and safe – outside someone else's room.

There was no getting away from it. I was ashamed. I had thrown an old, blind spider out of its home.

What had made me do this? Fear. It all came down to that same old fear that makes humans so aggressive and, even though I knew the enemy, I had still behaved badly because of it.

I thought about this fear that we humans have and which seems to rule our lives. Everywhere I look, I can see that people are afraid. I can understand that some sorts of fear are sensible, like when humans lived in caves or wherever they could and when everything around them was scary. They only had their own soft bodies and simple weapons then and there were wild things that would kill and eat them. Other humans would probably kill and eat them too. Nobody knew how natural events happened either. Lightning, storms, darkness – they were all mysterious happenings and scary.

Life is a bit easier than that lately though and it should have got better, but its different things that seem to scare people now and they still seem frightened a lot of the time. Things like fear of being cheated in some way, bested, or made to seem a lesser person than another. Fear that somebody might be getting more. Fear of not having enough money or possessions. Fear that they will lose the money or possessions that they do have. Fear that a loved one will come to harm. Fear that they, themselves, will come to harm. Fear of not being loved. Fear of being loved too much. Fear of this. Fear of that. Fear that makes a person hurt a big old spider that was only going about its business.

Every time I behave badly, I can trace it back to the fear of something. If I could stop being afraid of anything, I would be a much nicer person.

The Guesthouse was also a coffee shop and they asked if I would mind having breakfast early because, after that, they opened the shop. That suited me fine and it led to an amazing happening.

I had set off that little bit earlier than I would normally have been starting out and just turned down a small road leading to Wortley, when a cyclist approached me. As he got nearer, there was something familiar about him. Had I seen him cycling somewhere else? Then, a voice that I knew well said "Hello – its Pat!" and I recognised him. It was Rob, a good friend of mine, but he was trying to confuse me, for he had shaved off his beard. I had only ever known him with his beard attached, so that wasn't fair.

Rob had taken a few days off to go cycling. Today was mid-summer solstice, the longest day and he was seeing how far he could cycle during it. We sat and talked for a while. When we parted, anybody watching would have thought me a very forward walker, giving such a big hug to a cyclist apparently just met on the road.

If I had left either earlier or later, I would have missed meeting Rob, because it was only for a short distance we were covering the same bit of road. It was a remarkable co-incidence, our time lines crossing like that. I wondered how many such crossings we just miss? There might have been times when whole lives would have been changed by meetings just missed and we'd never know.

Anyway, this time, our lives could have been

234

changed for the worse, as we were sitting in a bit of a dangerous place on a blind corner, but we were lucky and went our opposite ways, happy at having met.

* * *

I was in the Cotswolds and the way was beautiful. The steep hills and hollows gave forth chocolate box and jigsaw puzzle views of little houses hidden away, peeping out at me and there was such a peaceful feeling from the rural scene. My only slight worry was that my left leg had become very painful on the shin in the place where I had had the trouble from the right leg. That other hurt had long since stopped and I had forgotten it, but this new pain worried me in case it got really bad like the other had. No vein had broken though, it was probably the constant pounding of the leg on tarmac. I still had no trouble at all with my feet.

I walked down a road that was no longer a road because it had been blocked off to traffic. There was grass growing in it now and it was covered in sheep droppings. Then I came into the most beautiful village of Horton. It was very quiet and peaceful, in fact, I didn't see a soul as I walked through. I looked in on the Church and sat in the graveyard for a while. It was even quieter there. Everybody was lying down, except for the ones in the cremation section, where the stones were close together. My daughter, when she was five, had seen these in a churchyard and asked "Mummy, why were those people buried standing up?"

I knew there was a hill fort somewhere nearby and one at Little Sodbury, where I was headed next. This countryside had been lived in for a long while but the word 'fort' didn't sound good news, like they had been fighting again.

As I walked towards Little Sodbury, I suddenly

decided to walk to Chipping Sodbury instead so, what I missed, I did not know.

Chipping Sodbury was a 'new town' where the building plots had been laid out on either side of the road. The original road had been diverted for this purpose. That was back in the 12th century though and the developer of that time was called William Crassus, known more popularly as William the Fat.

Sodbury seemed a very popular name. There was Little Sodbury, Little Sodbury End, Old Sodbury and Chipping Sodbury (the big one) and, as I walked over Sodbury Common, it was a pleasant way.

I liked Chipping Sodbury too. The kindness to me continued when a young man in a bakers gave me an extra cake 'on him'. The Information Centre told me of a B & B that wasn't on their list but they thought was at Pucklechurch. That was about five miles on and would get me into Bath with an easy walk the next day, so I launched myself off with hopes that I'd find it.

When I got to Pucklechurch, I couldn't find the B & B, but asked in a pub and, yes, the young man there did know of it and directed me there.

I found Ray in the garden. His wife Joy, was out and he wasn't sure they had room because she dealt with the bookings. I did hope that there was a space for me. Ray gave me a cup of tea and I looked around the lovely garden with him. He had a lot to look after, including a really good vegetable patch. The soil looked good, but it was all hard when you touched it, like clinker. A bit had come off the cultivator and we searched for it. I found it in long grass and was pleased.

When Joy came home, she said there was a room that her grandson had been using. He was away now, but if I didn't mind the sudden rearrangement, she would go and tidy it up. I certainly didn't mind and wouldn't have worried even if it had not been tidied. I was very grateful and had a lovely stay.

Joy had the same book of maps that mine had come from and wanted to see where I had walked. Boy, it did seem a long way. Even I was impressed!

That evening, the church bells were being rung, a lovely village sound.

The name Pucklechurch had seemed a strange one but, apparently, it was originally Purcela's Church, not that Purcela sounded much like Puckle to me. In Saxon times, it was an important place and poor King Edmund was trying to save his steward from being murdered by an outlaw called Leofa, when he got killed himself.

"I suppose you know you've just killed King Edmund!"

"Oh dear. I thought he was a serf."

"Well, you wait. You'll cop it and that will just serf you right."

The King was buried at Glastonbury and his successor Edwy gave the whole place to the monks, with Abson, Wick, Westerleigh and Doynton thrown in as well.

In return, they had to pray for his soul. Pretty good deal for the monks, I thought.

"Here you are, you can have East Grinstead for a prayer.

"Oh, ta very much. Tell you what, give us Forest Row and Copthorne as well and you can have an extra big prayer."

"OK. Do you want Gatwick tool?"

"No thanks. Useless bit of land that. Never be able to use it for much."

Next morning, Ray and Joy waved me goodbye as I set off on what was a fairly short walk to my friend Gladys. She lived on the Lansdown side of Bath and that was the part I would be reaching first.

My leg wasn't too bad. I had decided that I had slipped into the bad habit of thudding along flat footed, rather than using my ankles. That movement probably jarred the leg as it came down, so I made the effort to walk with a rocking heel to toe motion. It seemed to be working. When I'm walking on rougher ground I have to move my feet more, but on roads most of the time, it becomes easier just to 'thud'.

It was uphill for a long way to Lansdown, but I had plenty of time. I sat in Beckford Tower grounds for a while amongst the gravestones and it was very peaceful. I reached Gladys' house quite early. She had told me she would be out for a while in the afternoon, but had left the key for me, so I let myself in, had a bath, made myself tea and relaxed.

A friend is a true friend when you can let yourself into their house, use their bath and soap and help yourself in the kitchen. There was no doubt about this with Gladys. I knew I was welcome to do all these things and it was a good warm feeling, accentuated by having been away from personal friends for so long.

When Gladys came back, she found a clean, glowing and mellow person, sitting with feet up, drinking her tea and reading her paper.

It was so lovely seeing my old friend. We had known each other many years. I was sorry that she suffered bad health. She has not been right since a long flight to New Zealand and back many years ago and suffers such terrible discomfort in her legs that she gets hardly any sleep at nights. It's only recently that the long distance flight health risk has been recognised, but Gladys knew all about the effects a long time ago. She gets very tired. I wished I could wave a magic wand over her and cure it, but couldn't. It's sad to watch a friend suffer and be able to do nothing.

Our time together was far from sad though. We caught up with each other's news and had a happy evening. Next day I left reluctantly and Gladys waved me goodbye equally reluctantly, but the warmth of her remained with me as I walked on.

It was 23rd June now. I walked down a very steep hill into Bath and then up a very steep one out of it. The town of Bath sits in a basin of land and Gladys had told me that, with the hot springs underneath and it being situated like that, an inversion layer sometimes forms in summer and it gets a bit uncomfortable. She is pleased that she lives up much higher.

Despite my sadness at saying goodbye to my friend, my spirits lifted as I joined a little road which was deserted except for me and had grass growing in the middle.

I sat under a tree. Now, what can you say about looking down from under a leafy tree at beautiful countryside all around, studded with green fields and woods. Unless you've sat in such places yourselves you can perhaps imagine the picture, but not the feeling. Words are not enough to explain what its like. But, if you have sat by yourself, without chat, under the branches of such a tree, looking out at mellow English countryside, with the breeze of a million years brushing your face, then you know what I mean.

I joined the main road near Marksbury, which wasn't so good. Sometimes it had pavements, sometimes not. It was very busy because, in accordance with the Law of Sod, I had clashed with the Glastonbury Festival. Occasionally, a police car would cruise by me, surveying my totally respectable body and rucksack with more suspicion than I would have expected.

I decided I'd walked enough when I got to Chewton Mendip. King Alfred – you know, the one who burnt the cakes – put Chewton Mendip in his Will. I don't know who he was giving it to. It's a shame to be remembered for hundreds of years for a culinary disaster. Poor old Alfred. I have suffered from such an insult myself. One of my so-called friends once commented that my cooking came in two varieties – raw or burned. Well, that wasn't my fault. I was cooking on a Rayburn stove at the time, using wood as fuel. If the wind dropped suddenly, so did the temperature and, if my husband snicked in and put a plastic bag or dead rat in, then the temperature suddenly soared.

Another 'friend' said that my cooking improved in inverse proportion to the amount of time I spent on it. I took a few minutes on that one before I realised I'd been insulted and then I hit him with one of my cakes.

Watching how I walked and not plodding along flatfooted seemed to have worked on the leg because it had been OK, only starting up a bit at the end of the day. I reckoned it was not going to give any more trouble now. There was a B & B in the centre of Chewton Mendip. I knocked at the door. There was no answer. I asked about it at the shop. They said there was another one a bit further on, just out of the village. The people who ran these two places were relatives.

So, I walked on and knocked at the other place. No answer there either, but there was a church opposite that was now a house. It was beautiful and a gentleman was in the garden. He said the people at the B & B wouldn't be long because they had left the garage open. He said that there was another a mile further on. That was in the wrong direction to where I was headed the next day, but he said that, if I had no luck with this B & B, he would ring for me to see if they had a vacancy. That was very kind, but I waited a while and all came out well. The people came back and there was room for me. They had been out with the relative, which accounted for why neither had been in.

It was a cosy and comfortable place. The church house opposite was a very pretty view from my window.

I went for a walk in the evening and did some phoning. I phoned Gladys to thank her and say that I had found somewhere comfortable for the night. Then I phoned my sister and the news there was not so good. Mum had fallen in the kitchen and hurt her back as she fell. Nothing was broken, she had just strained the muscles. Anne sounded a bit stressed.

It had been a problem for quite a while, this 'blacking out' that poor old Mum was subject to. She would have practically no warning, except that she made a sort of funny face before it happened. If we were there and saw the funny face, we could catch her or, even better, guide her to a seat if we had time but often, she would just go down – crash! If she didn't hurt herself on the way down, she recovered quickly as if nothing had happened. It was a great worry for us but not very nice for her either!

It had been amazing that she had not hurt herself badly. The worst so far had been when she had fallen on the hard kitchen floor and broken her ankle and that had not been an easy time for any of us. Also, it was probably part of the reason I didn't sleep so well at home. Mum got up in the night and, I was instantly awake, half expecting to hear a 'thump' which meant she had blacked out and fallen. It didn't happen often, but enough to condition me to waking up at the least noise. On this walk, I had slept really well.

I was really sorry for Mum's pain and worried about it, but also, (no doubt selfishly but it was how I actually reacted), I felt the future coming towards me. In about three weeks, it would be my turn and my responsibility again. The next morning, I had a headache.

I walked to Wells. It wasn't very pleasant at first, on a road with so much traffic, but a pavement appeared about a mile before the town and, that was better. I walked down, down and still down, on a long hill into Wells.

I had been there before, when I'd walked from Bournemouth to Bath. That time, the night before walking into Wells, I had slept in an old barn on top of a hill. It had been deserted, clean, with no rats and a magical place in which to stop but, foolishly, I had trodden on a rusty nail, which had gone into the arch of my foot. I had some cheese with me, which had gone mouldy. "Ah!" I thought. "Penicillin." So I ate it. It seemed to do the trick, because the foot soon healed up, with no bad effects.

There were hordes of people in Wells, because of the Glastonbury Festival. Lots of police were around. It is very small but classed as a City with its beautiful Cathedral. It got its name from springs in what is now the Bishop's Garden, which gave forth fresh, clean water. The water was made available to everybody. It flows, to this day, in two small streams down each side of the main street, ignored now, but what a boon such a supply of water would have been in the past. The first thing to be thought of when people gathered to live together would have been the supply of fresh water.

Wells is beautiful. A tad too many people around but then, I was one of them, so had no right to grumble. I bought myself a very large milk shake and then took the long way round on beautiful country lanes which led in the direction I was headed.

Looking at the map, I knew that I was probably going to have to sleep out that night, but it was good weather, so no worry at all. The next night, I was going to stay with another friend. The day after that, I was going to meet Joyce in Taunton, who was coming out for a week's walking with me. We had thought we would be meeting much further up the country, but I had made better progress than I had expected and so was further down.

Taunton was the best place to meet her off a train. I had planned my walking so that I could get to Taunton by the 26th June. I had found it a bit difficult to find a meeting point by a certain date, but was so much looking forward to walking with Joyce for a while, that it was worth the effort. Meeting her came at just the right time, when I fancied the company of a friend for a while and I knew she was looking forward to coming.

I had to step out to complete the distance though. That day, I reckoned I had to walk about 18 miles to make sure I didn't have too long a walk the next day on my way to Colin.

I had originally planned to go through Glastonbury, where Joyce could also have joined me, but had no intention of doing that now with the festival on.

I had been fascinated by the grid-like roads and tracks marked on the map when I had previously looked at the area through which I was now walking and had wanted to see what it was actually like there. I would be walking through the Somerset Levels and could guess that it would be flat, drained marshland, with many dykes and waterways criss-crossing it. This proved to be correct.

I walked on almost deserted roads that stretched out in front and behind me for as far as I could see. Often there were willows edging them. Far off to my left I could see Glastonbury Tor, standing like a brooding sentinel. To the right and left was farmland that had been reclaimed from the marshes. It could have been boring, but I didn't find it so at all. I just walked on and on and my mind settled into the flat 'sameness' for miles, accepting it happily, much in the same way that I can work on a production line without getting bored.

I stopped on a bridge and looked both ways to where the waterway stretched out in a straight line to the far distance. There was a rhythmic whoosh, whoosh as swans flew over my head.

I reached Westhay, which wasn't very big, more a hamlet, but it did have a shop where I bought water because, looking around as I'd walked, the water didn't look as though it would be too good to drink even with iodine in it. There was plenty of it all right, but it was all a bit stagnant and not flowing fast.

Westhay had originally been called Westeie, where the 'eye' meant island, because once, it would have been just that, rising slightly above the ancient salt-marsh, which was drained during the middle ages.

For many years, peat has been dug all around and one peat cutter, a Mr. Ray Sweet, was digging away in 1970, when he found ancient waterlogged timber and a flint arrowhead. That was how the world's oldest known trackway was found. It was 6,000 years old and had been made of poles held by side-pegs. Turfs had strengthened it, so people could walk on it and cross the sedge and reed swamps. The track has been called the 'Sweet Track' after the peat cutter. It wasn't open to the public though, otherwise I should have like to have walked on this ancient way. It seemed amazing to me that a track of such an age could still be found.

Shortly after Westhay, I walked past the 'Peat Centre'. Next to it was a Garden Centre, which had a café, so I went in there first to indulge in tea and cake. Walking through, I felt a twinge of homesickness, because I often went to such places with my mother. You can usually get a wheelchair around those garden centres and there are beautiful plants and other interesting things for her to look at.

The feeling soon passed. There were only two ladies there and they asked if I was headed for the Festival because, if so, I was going in the wrong direction. They were not the first to point that out. A couple of times before, people had told me that I was going the wrong way!

I approached the building where there was a
display of peat moor wildlife. As I got near, a hand
appeared and turned the notice around to 'closed'. A man
in another building had watched this happening and
laughed. "Nothing personal" he said, "It just happens to
be closing time, but look around the iron age village for as
long as you like."

I hadn't realised there was one, but went through
the gate he indicated and there I was, in the middle of an
iron age village. It was great, built to how they thought
people lived then. There were even animal skins on the
beds. It looked quite cosy. I wouldn't have minded
staying the night there.

I remembered how, some years before, there had
been television coverage of some people who spent a year
living an iron age life. It had thrown light on some things
that had puzzled archaeologists. One had been the basin-
like indentations that always seemed to be found near the
doors of the dwellings. The modern iron-agers found that
these had been caused by chickens making dust baths.
One puzzle solved! It brought to mind though how easy it
would be to draw wrong conclusions.

I had once been picking raspberries in our farm
garden one evening, when the small girl from the cottage
next door came and chatted to me. Then she skipped off
because it was her bed time. Next morning, I was out
there again, picking, when the small one came out.
"Oooh, you've been picking raspberries all night!" she said
impressed. And nothing could convince her that I hadn't.
She had seen me last thing in the evening and first thing in

the morning and, both times, I had been picking raspberries. Therefore, it was logical and obvious that I had been doing that in between too.

People looking at things from the past often make that assumption. They observe discrete events and slurp them together in a way that seems obvious or suits them. There are fossils in a strata, then a gap, then more fossils. And we make assumptions about what happened in the gaps, like the little girl knew did the raspberries.

Who is to know that, in between meteorites landing, the dinosaurs were not playing flutes and taking ballet classes?

I left the iron age and walked on down the road, passing a mountain of peat at the side. A few million years were stacked up there. I started looking for a place to stop. Just before I reached Shapwick, I saw the place it was going to be. There was a cleared field, with round black polythene wrapped bales of grass-to-be-silage lying scattered around.

It was ideal. The weather was warm and looked to stay fine. I took myself off to a corner out of sight and set up my home on the sheltered side of one of the bales, making certain there was no chance of the bale rolling in my direction and flattening me beyond recovery. Around the edge of the field, the grass the baler missed had dried into hay, so I made a soft mattress of that under my sleeping bag.

I watched the sun setting behind the romantic black bales. Looking at them, I felt a bit of a wrench inside for the farm life I had once had, remembering the whole family setting to and getting the big round bales of silage in. It had been hard work then, because it was bags we put them in, no wrap-around cling film like now. Mike had made up a spike for the front of the tractor so that he could carry a bale on the front as well as on the back

In the meantime, before we could use the bags, the children and I had to check there were absolutely no holes in them. No air must get in or the grass would go mouldy instead of fermenting to a nice tasty cattle sauerkraut. It meant putting them right over our heads and getting inside, so we'd be able to see any pinpoints of light in the darkness if there were holes. It looked really funny from outside, like a giant black mushroom dancing about. We put tape on any holes we found.

Then, we had to get a bag on the bale. Sometimes it went on easily, sometimes the bale was on the large side and it was a real struggle. After that, we put an old bag on top to prevent wind damage to the important inner plastic. That bag had been on the floor before and was usually covered in mud and cow dung. Thankfully we didn't have to get inside to check for holes but, by the time we had finished for the night, we ourselves were almost as black as the bales and not smelling half as sweet.

It was peaceful in the field. I piled hay on top of myself and slept soundly through the night. It was the best time I had spent outside, warm and comfortable, even better than the straw barn.

There was heavy dew when I woke but, as the sun got higher, it soon dried.

Today I was making my way to Fivehead to stay with Colin. I had met him on a working holiday spent hedge laying a few months before, which he had been helping to lead and he had invited me to stay on my walk. I'd phoned a couple of days before to check it was all right and it was, so I was looking forward to meeting him again.

My leg had stopped giving me any trouble now and I passed through Shapwick, where the original John Bull came from. It was said that it was this John Bull who had written the National Anthem.

Not far from here, in 1685, the Battle of Sedgemoor took place, but it was a massacre really, by King James' gang against the rebellion led by the Duke of Monmouth. The rebels were aiming to march across the moor at night and surprise the King's men, but the local guide leading them lost the way and the confusion led to their detection and defeat. One man losing his way and history goes a completely different way than it would have done if he had gone in the right direction or stayed in bed. The thousands that died are still under there somewhere, lying where they were killed. I suppose it all helped to keep the population down.

I carried on past High Ham through a place with the most fascinating name of Huish Episcopi, where there was a most beautiful church. I asked a couple of people where the name Huish Episcopi came from, but they didn't know. To me, it sounded Roman.

It was a very hot day, but I could take it easy. I saw there was The Priest's House at Muchelney and fancied seeing it and went the long way round so that I could pass by there.

The countryside around me was different to yesterday. It was marked as moors on the map but was really farmland.

Quite naturally, when I got to Muchelney, the Priest's House was closed, which I didn't expect on a Friday in June but they must have known I was coming.

The Abbey was open though, so I went in. It had been there a long time. I walked around the part that had been built in the 1500s, which was old enough and very interesting, but outside, there were the ruins of the original Abbey, which dated back to 5-600AD. The lady at the ticket office was lovely and I talked to her for a while. She made people tea if they wanted. This person did want. Then I topped it off with an ice-cream, which I took outside and sat talking to a couple of ladies on holiday there. I enjoyed the chats very much.

On I went to Curry Rivel and then it was main road all the way to Colin's house, which was situated by the road I was walking along, so easy enough to find. It had not been very nice walking along that road, so I was pleased I'd avoided a bit of it by going via Mulcheny.

Colin was there, working on his land and it was great to see him again. He showed me around his smallholding. He is preserving old varieties of apples, which are in great danger of dying out, by grafting any that he can get hold of onto root stock. He had grown over 90 varieties in this way, with names I hadn't even heard of. Many would fruit for the first time that year. He was also growing willow, making an arbour from it and there was a wonderful old hedge with so many different things growing in it. He was caring for that hedge as old hedges should be cared for. He grew fruit and vegetables too.

There was a lot of work looking after all that. I didn't want to stop him from what he had to do, so went and picked raspberries, which he hadn't found time for, while he worked in the vegetable patch. I really enjoyed that.

I had learned that Joyce would be coming into Taunton at 10.30 in the morning and had planned to meet her and continue the walk, but Colin said we would both be welcome to stay over until the following day. I didn't want to be a nuisance, but could see that he really meant it and I knew that Joyce would love to stay.

Colin didn't have a car and I'd planned to go into Taunton by bus, but he said his neighbours were going and would most likely give me a lift which, bless their hearts, they did, dropping me off at the station in time for Joyce's train.

* * *

It was so marvellous to see Joyce. We were like two kids laughing together and had a relaxed time in town, shopping for the three of us. We were going to do the meal that night and Colin was risking the results.

We got a bus back easy enough. I knew Colin would get on with Joyce fine because you'd have to be trying really hard not to. I picked more raspberries for him to freeze and Joyce strung onions to hang and dry, as she had learned to do when she was young and staying with her grandmother in Wales. Colin had done a load of washing for me and it was dry and fresh to the nose. Storms had been forecast for the day and the sky certainly did look very black and threatening at times, but it never did rain.

Colin survived our cooking remarkably well, but it was with the help of lovely fresh vegetables from his garden so we couldn't really mess it up that badly.

Next morning, we found that It had rained in the night, so everything smelled fresh and green as we walked off in the morning. We had enjoyed our stay with Colin very much and he came a little way along the road with us. He pointed out how the main roads hereabouts ran along ridges. This was because it had been all marshland once and, in the past, the high ridges were the only places where it was possible to have a track or road that would be passable all the year. The marshes had mostly been drained over the past years but recently, there had been a back-lash against this draining and now, some had been put back to wetlands and were being allowed to flood naturally in the winter, as in times gone by.

Joyce and I were carrying enough food for the day and a bit more because I knew from looking at the map that we'd be out in the 'wilds'. It didn't seem to be tourist land where we were walking now, but the tourists didn't know what they were missing because it was surely beautiful. We walked through countryside of undulating hills, with woodland that had often been coppiced. The soil must have been good, because there were a lot of small market farms around and fruit growing too.

It was fun having Joyce there and we laughed along our way. Both of us love walking on little roads and these we were treading came from our best dreams. I was mindful of the fact that I had been walking for almost two months now and Joyce had just come out, so was not intending to make her walk too far. If we didn't want to encounter busier roads and built-up areas though, to get to where there would likely be accommodation would be too far a distance to walk comfortably, so we both expected to sleep out that night. Joyce had been warned and was quite looking forward to the adventure.

We passed through Hatch Beauchamp. The word 'hatch' was one I was used to because, on the Ashdown Forest near where I live, it relates to the places where there had been gates that let people into the Forest, for example, Colemans Hatch. That was in the days when it was a Royal Hunting area. Hatch Beauchamp apparently was the same. Hatch had meant a gateway into the ancient Neroche Forest, which had also been a Royal Hunting area.

"Shut that pesky gate. You'll let all the deer out

and the peasants in if you're not careful!"

This village was also at the start of the Blackdown Hills, an area that I decided I would most definitely like to explore further in the future.

We walked through Staple Fitzpaine, where the 'staple' was the standing stone near the Church. The stone, it is said, was thrown there by the Devil, (no reason given) and it bleeds if pricked with a pin. I had no intention of assaulting an innocent stone so I cannot verify if this is true or not.

Now, we were walking up high in the borderland between Somerset and Devon. We actually walked along with the border on our right for about 4 miles. It was cold and windy because we were up so high and clouds threatening rain collected ominously.

The people of the Blackdown Hills have not had a very good press in the past. There is the story of an old man who had not washed or changed clothes for seven years and who shared his food with the rats who lived with him. His logic was that, if he fed the rats, they wouldn't get hungry enough to eat him. Seemed sensible enough to me.

A rather spiteful story goes around of local farmers that, if they dropped eggs on the road, they would lick the remains up rather than let them go to waste. I wondered how many local farmers were in the habit of dropping eggs on the road. The stories are sad really, because it is obvious from them and the 'hardness' attributed to the people, that it was because of a great deal of poverty and hardship. It is all very well for people who are well fed and smug themselves to criticise.

As late as 1865, an evangelist ditched his plan to go to the West Indies and came to the 'Blackdowns' instead, because the people there were considered to be heathens and uneducated, more in need of his services than the people in the West Indies. I'm sure its different now but, walking along, we could see how hard it could have been living there and how cut off from the rest of the world it would have been.

We had walked a long enough way and it was time to stop. I was enjoying Joyce's company too much to want to kill her on the first day, so we started looking around for a place to set down our beds and heads.

First, we saw a hopeful place in woodland, but found it was near a car park and didn't fancy that. Car parks are subject to people parking there for romantic purposes and, if they decided to go for a stroll or whatever, it could be that they would stumble all over us in the night, which we didn't really fancy, so we moved on. Then, we saw an old caravan in a yard and wondered if the people in the house would let us stop there. The house was advertising alternative therapies so we thought that perhaps they would have a broad and open view of the world and might be sympathetic to our need for a shelter. We would have been happy to pay for it, but didn't get a chance to offer because we were given a rather brusque 'brush off'.

Agreed that I probably was doing a pretty good imitation of a tramp but Joyce looked almost respectable and I had pushed her forward to be seen first, but to no avail. Obviously the alternative lifestyle on offer was only theoretical.

So, off we went, still looking for a place and getting more and more tired. Then, Joyce spied a field full of silage bales. There were several trailers in the field. One trailer was right at the edge, up against a bank and was sheltered on all but one side. It had obviously been there a long time, because grass was growing on top. The sleeping accommodation looked ideal to me, with plenty of room for both of us underneath and a roof above. The bank went up steeply at the back, we couldn't be seen from the road, so it felt very snug and secure.

We set up home and cooked ourselves soup and coffee. Joyce had kindly brought out more fuel blocks for me. Then we sat near the silage bales in the last of the sun. The latest fashion seemed to be very pale green or white plastic covering the bales, instead of the black I was used to seeing. On this field, they had some of each. I felt them. The black ones were very warm indeed to the touch, but the pale ones were cold. I wondered what difference that would make to the quality of the silage inside.

Looking at what Joyce had brought for sleeping out, I was a bit dubious because it wasn't the waterproof bag I thought she had borrowed from her son, but a large sheet of polythene and an ordinary sleeping bag. Her son had assured her that it was warm sleeping out at this time of year. That was probably true for him because he was able to sleep out in quite cold weather and be warm. Men seem to keep much warmer than women in general, but I had always found I was seldom warm, whatever time of the year I chose to sleep out. However, Joyce fastened the polythene up around her like a little tent and it looked like it could be all right.

We lay down under our shelter. I lay on my back and looked up. There was a large hole in the floor of the trailer, neatly placed above my face. I muttered, Joyce laughed and I moved down a bit to avoid the hole, because it looked like it was going to rain.

We tried to doze off. There was only the one side that was exposed to the elements. It should have been cosy under there, but I'm sure the wind must have changed direction. It certainly got up more strength because soon, there was a strong and bitter blow of very cold air engulfing us, as the wind blew directly under the trailer.

The polythene sheet was not a great success as it was very uncontrollable and made a loud noise flapping in the wind. Joyce soon became very cold. I was more used to it and, although I felt uncomfortable it certainly wasn't anything near so cold as when I was up in Scotland. I had placed my rucksack so that my face was sheltered from the blast.

"Aargh" The interesting sound between a squeak and a gurgle came from Joyce. She had put her hand up to her hat to pull it down more firmly and had encountered a slug, which was sitting on top of it.

"Its so *** cold that even the slugs are coming in to get warm!" said Joyce.

She flung the slug away. She didn't admit to flinging it in my direction but, if she didn't, then a near relative of the creature got the same idea because, shortly afterwards, I put my hand up to pull the bag more around my ears and the hand encountered a large slug about to crawl over my face. That one took to flying as well, but I really can't state in what direction.

I was worried about Joyce getting too cold, but morning came with both of us rising groggily for hot drinks. It was obvious that it would not be a good idea to sleep out with just that polythene sheet unless it got very much warmer so we would have to find accommodation at nights. Joyce said that she'd had a mental image of sleeping under the stars on a balmy summer night not, as she aptly put it, "Under a ruddy trailer with a bitter wind blasting in on me all night and slugs in my hat!" Well – what do you expect for one-star accommodation? It was cheap.

Before I started the walk, other people had thought of joining me at some time. They had formulated some idea that it would be an organised walk of a reasonable length every day, ending up at a nice comfortable place of accommodation. They had no idea! Lucky for them perhaps that they didn't come.

We were really laughing as we walked off, especially about the slug. Joyce said there was probably one inside her hat at this very moment, hitching a lift. Quite naturally, about a mile further down the road, we saw a hay barn which would have suited us much better. That's the trouble. You never know, when you see somewhere not fantastically comfortable but where you could reasonably stop, whether there would have been a better place ahead. Maybe, there would, or maybe there would be nowhere else for miles, so you just have to do your best with what crops up.

We were cold at first but soon warmed up with the walking and the weather was beautiful. We walked on a bridle-way over Sampford Moor, meeting some horse-persons who looked at us a bit quizzically, obviously wondering where on earth we had sprung from to be walking over the moors so early with rucksacks on our backs.

We stopped and made some coffee but, shortly after that, joined the main road and came across a tea caravan parked in a lay-by. Joyce didn't want anything and I wasn't going to bother, but she nagged me into having a bacon sandwich because she said I had got too thin. Just because I could squeeze through a gate now without opening it! I didn't put up a very strong argument against the bacon sarnie though.

We crossed the M5 and branched off at Sampford Peverell, walking along the Grand Western Canal. It was a really beautiful walk by this small Canal. There didn't seem to be any boats on it where we joined, for it was narrow and covered with water lilies. We had plenty of rests on the way, because we only had about 12 miles to walk that day into Tiverton. Perhaps the Canal route made it a couple more miles than that, but it was so pleasant. At least we should be able to get comfortable lodging at Tiverton. I had avoided killing Joyce on the first day, but probably only just and didn't really want to kill her on the second either.

We cut through Halberton to avoid a large loop in the Canal and got some food at a shop there. Then, we rejoined the Canal for more pleasant walking, right through to Tiverton. At the Canal's end, there was a very pretty café and we had a clotted cream tea.

I love clotted cream. When we were evacuated to a farm in Devon during the War, we had thick clotted cream on bread for breakfast every morning. The farmer's wife used to put a huge pan of fresh Jersey milk on the Aga cooker overnight and the very gentle heat caused the cream to float on the top in clots. In the morning, she would scoop it off. Sometimes, my sister and I would take milk from the top of the churn to drink and that would have cream lumps in it too and be warm from the cow. If Bill, the farmer saw us standing near the cow he was milking, he would milk 'squirt, squirt' into the bucket and then a squirt directly at us, when we would run away squealing. My memories of the time we lived at that farm are very happy ones. Being there gave me a taste for the countryside and definitely a strong taste for clotted cream. When the War ended and we had to return to town life, I never did get used to it and never got any clotted cream either.

As we were sitting at a table stuffing our faces, I saw that a small boy at a table next to us was staring and staring at me, with wide open eyes. When I went into the 'ladies' I looked into the mirror and could see his point. I did look a bit as if I had just come from out of the jungle, tanned and with wild grey hair, which looked almost white against the suntan. Joyce was still reasonably dapper and, when she walked along, everything was neat. When I walked along, there were articles dangling everywhere, like wet clothes and trainers hanging out to dry, water bottle, map – just everyday necessary things.

We were both fairly tired as we got into Tiverton despite the shorter distance because we had not had much, if any, sleep the previous night and had started off very early. 'Information' directed us to a place at Canal Hill. This was back in the direction we had just walked from, at the end of the Canal. We had only just missed seeing it and, if we had asked the lady at the café, she would have directed us there. But – we had found it in the end.

Pat and David gave us a terrific welcome. It was a beautiful rambling house and they had done a great deal of work on it. Dave was recovering from an industrial injury and they had both been having a hard time, but you would never have guessed that from their great sense of humour. Our stay with them was pure fun.

Joyce was whacked and in bed, slumbering peacefully by 7.30, but I stayed up and chatted with Pat and Dave, drinking Horlicks and laughing a lot.

In the morning, I stepped out of bed – and straight on to my friend Mr. Slug! I couldn't believe that. We were too high up for the slug to have crawled all the way up the outside wall, so there was only one reasonable explanation. Although we had joked about it, this slug really had hitched a lift. My rucksack was nearby, so I must have carried it for the whole day. What a cheek!

As I threw it out of the window, Joyce said, "Is it dead?" "Well, it might be able to fly," I replied. I seemed to be making a habit of throwing small creatures out of upstairs windows, but in this case, I didn't feel bad about it because I had trodden very firmly on the slug and was pretty certain it hadn't survived, because I seemed to have half of it still on my foot. And anyway, it didn't live here, so I hadn't thrown it out of its home.

The previous evening, I had mended the rip in my trousers that the barbed wire had caused in the Peak District, because the tear was threatening towards indecency. Joyce had been very co-operative in this and willingly donated a pair of silky knickers, which provided a nice lightweight patch that would dry quickly when the trousers got wet or were washed.

Dave teased Joyce for having taken to bed so early. It was not surprising though that she'd been tired – thrown suddenly as she had been into the walk, which had been fairly long when carrying a rucksack, on both days. Also, it must be said, but kindly, that Joyce is vertically challenged. In simpler language – she is a short-arse and so her little legs go one and a half steps for my one. We know that, because we tried it out and that means they do 50% more work than mine.

As a parting gesture, Dave had put notes saying 'left' and 'right' in our shoes, just to make sure we got it right.

It had rained very heavily at night, but had eased off by the time we left. All day, it drizzled, but never very heavily. It was warm and muggy though, so quite uncomfortable having to wear the waterproofs.

The day consisted of steep ups and downs, along beautiful country lanes. I could see views often, but Joyce, walking below the hedge-line, could not and had to wait for gate openings to be able to see further than the hedges. The after-rain smells were fresh and delicious. We passed one beautiful old rose that wafted perfume over us as we walked by.

These high hedges reminded me so much of those War years in Devon. My mother used to go out in the morning before she went off to work and scatter coloured breadcrumbs on the spiders' webs, so that later, when me and my sister walked down the lane, we would see the coloured webs and think it was the fairies that had been there. The spiders probably thought it was a damn nuisance.

My mother does have a magical turn to her. She used to write small letters to us, almost too small to read and pretend they were from the fairies. I'm sure she believed in the fairies herself.

At Black Dog, I phoned husband in memory of a certain black dog we had known. He was pleased to hear that we had both met up successfully and were well and happy.

We would soon be crossing the Two Moors Way. I knew the area because the previous year I had done that beautiful walk, over Dartmoor, cross-country and finally over Exmoor. The weather had been terrible, rainy and cold, but I had enjoyed it.

Now, Dartmoor was looming up at us, grey and foreboding in the rain. This time, we would not be walking on it, but it brought back memories of how I had enjoyed the walk across it. I had been alone then and people had regaled me with horror stories of bogs swallowing up lone walkers such as myself, so I had been careful to avoid the bright green patches. The moor was bleak it was true, but also very beautiful. I had followed a line of stones that lead to a longstone and wondered about them. The stone lines on Dartmoor were very old and often went on for a long way. The ones I was following seemed to be on reasonably dry land so I supposed that was what they were originally there for – to show people the way, so that, even in mist and fog you would be walking on the drier land, not get lost and not be in danger of sinking in the bog.

I had walked then past ancient burial mounds and barrows. There were carefully placed stones all over the land and I had heard that once, there used to be many more, but they had been removed. I had had a vision then, of the whole of the British Isles being covered with such stones and lines. There would have been much more forest than cleared land in those days, but I seemed to see that, wherever there were clearings, these stones had been erected. It must have been such a big part of the structure of the peoples' lives and included in everything they did. Maybe, there would have been special stones for certain purposes, but there were many others too all over the land, not just in special places for special times, but part of everyday life. It had been fun to wonder about all this as I had walked.

Having done that Moors walk, I knew where we were headed that evening. The previous year, I had stopped with a Community at Beech Hill who acted also as a basic lodging for travellers such as myself. I had arrived there, tired and soaking and received a kind welcome. I had sat around a log fire and dried my socks, which led to great happiness. Simple things make a lone walker very happy and dry socks is one of them. I knew that we would not be turned away this time either and, nor were we.

We had a room to ourselves at Beech Hill and could use the kitchen. We had just enough food left for the evening and breakfast. I met up with Connie, who remembered me from the previous year and me her. Connie's daughter had been expecting a baby when I was last there and now I met the nine month old actuality – a delightful bouncy boy.

I can sympathise with Communities and the people I have met in them have been kind and caring, but I'm not sure I could live in one. The fault lies, not in the Community, but my own temperament. If I had grown up with people all around me, perhaps I should like it, but my sister and I were by ourselves mostly and I never got used to folk around all the time. Now, I have many friends and enjoy it but the old pattern, once established is hard to break and I need to disappear and be completely by myself at times.

So - life surrounded by people all the time would just drive me nuts. I know that, in theory, a person can have their 'own space' in these communities but, from my experience of them when I have sometimes stayed in one for a longer time, it doesn't really work like that. There is always someone with a crisis or problem and, by the nature of the community, it is hard not to be involved also. That's not to say I don't care when people have problems, I do, almost too much at times, but it seems to be pretty constant and sometimes, if there are too many people with troubles, I find it gets a bit hard. Then, if it's possible, I run away for a bit to be by myself and come back refreshed.

The system of communes does give many people of the right nature a good life though, with others. You couldn't die unnoticed or be unhappy and have nobody care. This particular community had felt good before when I was there and it did now.

* * *

The lovely little lanes, with their steep hills continued. We by-passed Morchard Bishop and were too early for the shop to be open anyway. Connie had told me that there had been a change since the previous year, for one of the two shops had closed. Regulations and red tape had defeated the owner in the end.

This was the story all along my walk. Where there had been a village shop, now there was none. It had made it hard to get supplies sometimes and must be very difficult for those of the local people who have not got a car.

We had only had a small breakfast and were getting hungry. We saw two young men working on a roof and Joyce said we could mug them for their sandwiches. That thought sent us into peals of laughter and got some very strange looks. There might be a shop at Monkokehampton, but that was 10 miles along.

We reached Zeal Monachorum and sat in the church porch there. We were really in need of some food by now. It wasn't so much that I felt the need in my stomach, but I was beginning to feel weak, so knew I was hungry. Joyce just felt the truth – downright hungry! She suggested that, if we put two packets of coffee mix into the mug instead of one, it would be like a soup and more satisfying. I did this, making up two lots for each of us. It worked quite well and our bodies stopped complaining quite so much.

We walked on, round a corner and, blow us - there, come upon suddenly and completely unexpected, was a shop. Even more remarkable, it was open!

The lady at the shop made us up some really good sandwiches and we bought loads more food. I asked her where the name Zeal Monachorum came from. Was it Roman? She said no, it had meant either a Monk's Cell, or an Animal Pound. The two seemed to be a little bit different to me, but anyway, it was apparently a very ancient name. She also told us that somebody famous had recently called in to the shop on a walk such as ours. I can't remember who it was because I didn't know the name but I didn't admit that. Joyce knew of him, so that was all right.

After leaving the shop, as soon as we could stop, we sat and stuffed our faces and felt much stronger. Later, we sat by a bridge to have our official lunch.

It was lovely sitting there, peaceful and quiet, with the flowers of a cottage garden next to us. Suddenly, we heard the sound of something big coming closer and closer. The noise got very loud. I thought it must be farm machinery of some kind, because we were way out in the country on very small lanes.

It hove into view then and we couldn't believe our eyes. For a paralysed minute, we just stared because, what was coming over the bridge, taking up the whole road, was a road-sweeper! You know the sort, with brushes on one side, marching down the kerb and sucking all the rubbish up from the gutter. Except that here, in the middle of the countryside, there was no kerb, no gutter and no rubbish.

A cloud of earth and dust came along with the sweeper and settled on our rucksacks, sandwiches and us. We came to life rapidly then and removed ourselves and everything else from its reach very smartish.

The road-sweeper swept by and then, just in front of us stopped, reversed round an intersecting lane and came back again! The man driving it didn't even look at us or smile. It was like an inanimate monster from another dimension, taking samples from the dirt at the edge of the lane. It had almost taken samples of us too.

The huge machine lumbered on, filling the lane, and disappeared from whence it came. We sat there, with the dust settling around us, clutching our rucksacks and sandwiches to our bosoms, stunned for a while. Joyce said, "I don't believe what just happened," and then we laughed and laughed, for quite a long time.

We reached Monkokehampton, with full bellies and no further incidents. I had been sure there would have been somewhere to stay, but there was not. It was lucky indeed that we had found our shop because, although there was a shop at Monkokehampton, it followed the usual pattern of early-closing day being the one I had arrived there and was shut.

There was a choice of giving Joyce another cold and uncomfortable night or walk further to Hatherleigh. The second option seemed the best so, on we walked.

As we walked into Hatherleigh, there was a B & B right there. "Oh good," we thought, "Just what we need," but it was full. We walked to the centre and, there was another. There was no answer to our knock. Joyce was surprised at the fact there was no answer, but I was pretty used to it by now.

I had originally expected accommodation to get easier the further south I went, because there was much more of it but that had not proved to be the case, because it was into holiday time and often fully booked. Also, when I was by myself, sometimes people would not let a twin room to a single person because later on, they might get two people wanting it.

Joyce was also amazed at the lack of village shops and the difficulty of getting food. When we walk as a little group, it is usually on set footpath routes where many people walk and so it is easier with more accommodation and even tea-rooms. My route had been just as it went, often not where tourists passed by which was much more interesting as it happened. I might not have had the shops and tea-rooms this way, but I had seen many parts of my country that I should not have done if I had stuck to the popular trails.

I was surprised that, in all this time of walking, often on similar looking lanes, I had never got bored. No so far anyway and I was so near the end that I didn't think boredom would engulf me now.

I was so respectably far down the country by this time that, when they learned of my walk, people had stopped looking at me pityingly. They were even looking impressed or, sometimes, disbelieving. Before, when I had not yet gone very far, you could see that often, they had wished me well, but were a bit dubious that I'd make it. For myself though, except in the event of severe personal injury or Mum being ill enough for me to have to go home, I never doubted for a minute that I'd not finish the walk.

Anyway, here we were in Hatherleigh with the regular difficulty. A gentleman, even more elderly than ourselves, was walking by. We asked him if he knew when the people at the B & B we were standing next to would be back, or if there was anywhere else we could stay. He said that he thought the people had family illness at the moment and that was probably why they were away and no, he didn't really know of anywhere else. But, he said that we could stay with him! He just had to deliver some medicine that he'd got for a friend who couldn't get out and then he'd take us home.

He did too. This was Gordon and what a lovely person he was. His wife had died the previous autumn and he missed her so much. He said how kind people had been to him, but we could see that he was kind to people too, helping where he could.

We had a great time with Gordon. We treated him to a meal at his local pub, although I must say, Joyce and me ate the most. Joyce took off early to bed and I sat and chatted. Gordon had done so many interesting things. He was fighting Rommel in the desert while I was a small thing and was soon going for two weeks to Normandy with his family to visit the war museums there. He'd been a postman for many years. I found it hard to believe that he was now 77 because he didn't look even near that age and still did so much, working some of the time and helping others. He was Cornish and had only lived in Hatherleigh for three years but had made many friends and I could understand why.

We slept in Gordon's spare room, Joyce in the bed and me on my self-inflating mattress on the floor. Gordon had said that one of the things he was not very good at was seeing to himself food-wise but, bless his heart, he had set out a wonderful breakfast table for us, with such care and love. He had gone out and bought some marmalade especially for us.

Gordon's house was next to the abattoir, but we never would have known that. Such things are accepted by people in rural areas as a natural part of a way of life that has been going on for centuries. It's the 'townies' that get a bit precious about it all.

Outside his house was a tap, with natural spring water flowing out from it all the time. He said it had been used as drinking water for hundreds of years and, although the council had put up a sign saying not to drink it, he always used that water for drinking because he considered it much more pure than the 'treated' stuff coming out of the taps. He certainly didn't look bad on it, so we willingly filled our water bottles.

We walked off happily, warmed by our stay with Gordon. There was rain in the air all day but it never came to much. It was a good walk, with lovely scenery but naturally lots of hills. The next place there might be accommodation available was Lydford, which was a long walk for Joyce. I was worried about that because, on the way, she didn't look so well and, from her increasing disappearances, it was pretty obvious she had a bug of some sort. She wondered if it had been the water but I doubted that because I was perfectly all right and it seemed much more likely it was something that she had contracted before because the incubation period and type of problem suggested it more likely. However, it obviously would not be good for her to sleep out, so there was no choice but to do the distance.

After a while, we stopped and sheltered in an empty barn. I had intended to make us a drink but, when I looked for the enamel mug in which I boiled the water and out of which I drank, it was not there. Joyce had brought one with her, but it was plastic, so we couldn't boil water in it.

It was no use looking. I pulled everything out of my rucksack, saying loud and bad things, but it was not there. I remembered putting it into the bag and then checking around the room to make sure I had not left anything. The likely explanation was that it had fallen out of my bag when we had bought food at a shop before we started walking and I had opened the bag to pack the food away. I was so cross. Not only did it mean we couldn't have a drink, but I should have liked to have kept that mug as a memento of my walk.

The trouble was, I had not been concentrating. By myself, I find I'm very methodical and think more clearly what I am doing but, with other people, I chat away and my concentration goes. It happens all the time and is not their fault, but my own. I don't have to chat when I should be concentrating. I think that part of the problem is that, when I'm by myself, I only have me to rely on and so have to take total responsibility. Therefore, I take great care. When I'm with someone else, I subconsciously relax, thinking that in some way, the responsibility is now shared but of course, there is absolutely no reason why they should be responsible for me not losing my possessions!

I certainly become more careless though when I am with others, I've noticed it before. I'm a bit like Pooh, the bear of little brain. I can only think of one thing at a time and should know that by now.

Joyce just kept her head down while the things were flying around. She knows me well enough to realise that any anger expressed is not directed against her but anger at myself for being so stupid and she also knows it passes over like a thundercloud. Often she makes me laugh at myself and then, the blue sky reappears even more quickly.

We reached Lydford, which we had expected to be a centred type of village, but was more like strip development from more ancient times. We were too tired to walk to Lydford Castle, which was only ruins anyway. I'd seen ruins before and didn't want to make one of Joyce!

The castle had a bit of a reputation though. In Saxon times, there were nasty laws against anybody who mined tin illegally and lots of offenders were put to death rather painfully and unpleasantly on Gallows Hill.

I didn't see it for myself but heard that, in the old churchyard, there was a tombstone to a watchmaker. It says:

"Wound up in hopes of being taken in hand by his

maker and of being thoroughly cleaned, repaired and set going in the world to come"

Perhaps I should have an up-to-date version put on my tombstone. It could be much simpler (and cheaper) and just state "Hardware malfunction".

Surprise, surprise. It was a hassle to find somewhere to stay. Places were full. We got to the garage and shop, where people had told us there were two more B & Bs opposite each other, just up the road. I left Joyce and my rucksack at the shop and walked up to them. One was being done up and so was temporarily closed. At the other B & B, there was a very kind lady, who said that usually, she had plenty of room but today, six fishermen had booked in. The pub did accommodation though, she said and phoned to see if there was room. There was and so she reserved it for us.

I was happy at first because there was a pub opposite where I had left Joyce and I thought it was the one she meant but it was not to be that easy. It turned out that the pub was another one that was a mile and a half in the opposite way to where we were going the next day and already, we had walked some way in the wrong direction.

Normally, I would have called it quits, got food at the garage shop, walked back in the direction I would be taking the following day and found a place to sleep out, but I could tell that Joyce wasn't feeling too good. The lady though, hearing of our predicament, was so very kind. She drove down to the garage, and then drove both of us to the pub. We were very grateful to her.

I was still concerned though, because Joyce has a bad reaction to even a small amount of cigarette smoke and pubs are known for such a thing. I don't like the smoke either, but don't feel actually ill like Joyce and can tolerate it. She's better than any smoke alarm ever invented. If there is one person anywhere at one end of a house having a secret 'ciggy' and she is at the other end, she can detect it. They should train her for drug detection and employ her at airports!

Anyway, our room in the Fox & Hounds was good and not smoke ridden. We were happy to be comfortable and had a lovely view from our window. We phoned Gordon to tell him where we had got to. Next morning, the chef from the pub kindly drove us down to the garage, so we were only a half-mile out of our way, which was nothing.

It was rugged and beautiful country we now walked through. We passed Lydford Gorge and I should rather have liked to see that, but we'd managed to book ahead at a Guest House at Callington, so had to get along and anyway, we were far too early. It was not open for visitors until later in the morning.

We chatted happily and did well until getting on for mid-morning. Then, we saw a remarkable church up high at Brent Tor. It was so interesting and our heads were swivelled to the left so much, that I completely missed the very small lane at Brent Tor where we should have branched off.

This was the first time I had done anything like that. I had got lost through not being able to find the way, but never just walked by a road that was clear enough, because usually I checked in a quite neurotic way at each intersection to see where I was. I was always checking my compass too and should have soon seen that I was walking the wrong way, but this time, I was talking!

On we went, ignorant of my mistake and the road was very busy and not pleasant to walk along.

"Oh," said Joyce. "What's the town on our left?" I didn't think there should be one so just grunted. Then, shortly afterwards, she said, "We're in Tavistock!"

"Don't be silly." I said, in my best bossy voice.

"We are"

"We can't be – it's miles out of our way."

Then Joyce settled the dispute by saying, "Well, there's a sign saying 'Tavistock' in front of us," and, sure enough, there was and we were.

I realised then what I had done and was very, very cross at myself, not at Joyce. But it made no difference who I was cross at, I started to walk very quickly. Joyce says I do this when I am cross. I didn't know that I did it before she pointed it out, but must admit that she fell behind a bit.

I reached a phone box and stopped because, by then, I'd decided what to do. I had no intention of walking back up that busy road for miles. I'd phone for a taxi, to take us to where we should have been.

Joyce caught me up, puffing and trying not to laugh at me, but I'd regained some sort of composure with the formulation of the new plan.

I got a couple of taxi numbers from the phone box, Joyce saw one on a taxi going by and a lady passing gave us another two.

I phoned the first. "Too busy," said a woman's voice abruptly and hung up. I phoned two more and got the same reaction. My code number didn't seem to work in this phone box and I'd run out of change. Then, Joyce made a suggestion. "They won't pick people up from telephone boxes," she said, "because they assume it's a hoax call."

"There's an empty house a few doors along," said she. "Give them that number and the street."

Our luck changed. My code started working and, with our new "address", the next taxi office accepted us but said it would be an hour before they could come.

So we had lunch, which we'd carried with us and then, nearer the time, waited outside the house, with me worrying in case the taxi didn't arrive. The only alternative then, would be to walk to Callington by the busy main road and miss out on some very beautiful countryside. I didn't want to do that.

The taxi did arrive after an hour and the physical rest had probably done us good.

I showed the taxi driver where to drop us off and

he said he knew it well but, after he'd gone and we'd started walking, I realised that he'd put us down at the wrong intersection, so he hadn't known it that well after all. It didn't matter all that much though, because we could walk diagonally and rejoin where we should have been.

I was right not to miss this bit of the walk. We were now in the Tamar Valley and it was stunningly beautiful. Both of us vowed to come back and explore the area more thoroughly, giving it the time it deserved.

Then came a momentous stage in my journey.

At Horsebridge, we crossed the River Tamar and – I was in Cornwall! Joyce took a photo of me standing by the sign, looking very smug indeed.

I still had a way to go because it was a fair old step along the length of Cornwall, but this was the last county. Now, it would take something really bad to stop me. If I broke a leg, I reckoned I'd carry on, dragging it behind me.

The trials and tribulations of earlier in the day fell away from me and I walked light-hearted amongst the beauty of the wooded hills. I noticed that now, the trees were talking in Cornish and I couldn't understand what they were saying. Cornwall was unexplored territory for me and I had a feeling I would like it a lot.

Walking on, I felt very happy that I had been able to share such an important moment with a good friend.

* * *

The villages in the Tamar area were very small, but at one, we found a shop. When we went inside, there wasn't much for sale. I bought a can of drink but Joyce just wanted water, so asked if the lady would be kind enough to fill her bottle. At this request, the shopkeeper lady, who had been eyeing us with some trepidation, looked absolutely terrified. She took out her keys and locked everything within sight that needed locking before going out to the back to fill Joyce's bottle. We hadn't realised that we looked quite that scary, but I'd heard her talking to a man in the shop before she attended to us and it sounded as if she was getting out, which would account for there not being much on offer. I wondered if she'd had a bad experience, a hold-up or something, because she was certainly very wary of us.

It was a Post Office too there. Maybe that will be another one that is going to be closed up. A Post Office business must be very vulnerable to robbery and threat though. I hadn't thought about that before, how the poor small shopkeepers, as well as finding it hard to make a living, often become victims.

As the euphoria wore off, I realised that Joyce was not feeling at all well. She had not been well the previous day, but now she seemed worse. Earlier, she had quite severe indigestion and it had progressed to a badly upset stomach and she had to keep disappearing behind a bush. We hadn't ended up walking very much longer through my earlier mistake, but we had a long hard climb up to Kit Hill and I realised it was making her suffer considerably. At least we knew we had a place to go to and it wasn't so far ahead, but I was worried.

The walk up to Kit Hill had been beautiful. We had noticed ruins of chimney stacks all along, which I supposed had marked where the old mines had been. The monument at Kit Hill was a Mining Monument – an 85ft high stack, where the Miners used to meet for their 'Parliament'. It was tin that they had mined. King Egbert was up here in AD835, beating up the Britons and Danes.

We reached the top of the granite outcrop and the view was fantastic in all directions. You could see as far as Dartmoor in one direction, Bodmin Moor in another and the Eddystone Lighthouse in yet another. We couldn't see the lighthouse, but could see the moors. There are apparently old mine workings in the heather so a person has to be a bit careful as to where to put a foot. On a good day, such as we had been lucky with this day, it was truly beautiful. Joyce seemed to be feeling a bit better too.

It was only a couple of miles more into Callington, which was a nice town. I had originally planned to go nearer Bodmin, but had now organised to get to Liskeard, where Joyce could catch a train on a direct route home at the end of her week, so Callington hadn't been in my mind. I was pleased to encounter it though.

We arrived at our Guest House, which was very nice. The flowers outside were a picture. Walking down the road, there had been very attractive murals painted on walls. Altogether, I felt happy there and I was relieved that Joyce could stop and have a rest.

The next day was only nine miles into Liskeard and so we could have a half-day there just relaxing together. That would be good. I knew it had been tough for Joyce and felt a bit bad about that, especially as she was not well. I suppose I was a bit out of practice at having to be concerned about another person's welfare, having only had my own body to be concerned about. I had found it a bit of a responsibility and worry that she was ill, but there hadn't been a lot I could do about it if we were to carry on although sometimes we had had to walk extra miles to get to accommodation which I would not have done.   All in all, I had really enjoyed her company and appreciated how she had been willing to share part of my experience of walking. It did make me realise though that, if I embarked on any more such 'survival' walks, it is best to go alone because I do not want to kill my friends!

I had asked Joyce if I was any different to walk with than I usually was when on our more normal walks, or with a group. She put it politely, but said I was a bit 'remote' at times. I think the grumpiness scale was about the same, but that wouldn't have worried her.

I thought that Joyce deserved a medal for putting up with a week on my walk, especially as I had been walking for 2 months and she had come out without having had all that practice. I could have made her a medal out of tin, as there must have still been plenty of that about.

* * *

We walked mostly on small lanes and arrived in Liskeard about mid-day. On the way, we had stopped at St.Ive, where teas were being served by the WI at the Church there. It was an old Church site there because the Knights Templars had been there way back in 1180.

It would have been so rural around St.Ive in 1180. I wondered what the Knights Templar people would think if they came back to see the wide tarmac of the A390, carrying all those metal dragons roaring their way by. I'd often thought that, if people from long ago could return and be gently introduced into modern life by sitting in a back garden with a washing line, well, that would have been remarkable enough to them for a start. The colours of the clothes and everything else around them would amaze and dazzle, The ordinary people in those days would have worn very drab colours. The cows would look a bit strange too, because very few are wearing horns of any colour nowadays.

I really enjoyed the tea and cake supplied by the WI. Their cakes are always delicious and so is their company. I had a lovely chat with a couple of people there while Joyce looked around the stalls. I didn't dare even look, but Joyce was going home the next day and could risk buying something that needed carrying. I'd had quite enough of carrying the extra weight of slugs with me.

When we got to Liskeard, we had another tea and cake stop. Life was indeed bearable.

Initially, it was the same old trouble to get accommodation but, in not too long a time, we had settled ourselves at a Guest House, where we got a very friendly welcome.

Joyce said that she had really fancied somewhere comfortable and cosy on her last night. Did she fear I was going to make her sleep at the railway station? I had muttered about the station being on the outskirts, and so probably reasonably isolated, with a nice little waiting room and had found that very tempting!

Anyway, we were surely comfortable and cosy at this place and had plenty of time after settling in to go back into Liskeard and explore a bit.

That night, I unloaded some of my things on to Joyce. She had suggested that, as I had only four more days to go, I could make my rucksack lighter and I thought this was a good idea. The weather had turned fine and warm, so I didn't think I needed my waterproof trousers, or spare trainers. Also, I'd lost my mug so I might as well give up the stove equipment too. There were many more places to get tea from now on and, if I slept out, I could make do with water.

I thought that, as the weather was so much warmer, I might be able to sleep out comfortably and save a bit of money.

I was hoping there would be time to finish this walk because there had been a TV programme about Nostradamus and his prediction that the world would end the next day, which was 4th July. Steve and Suzanne had been married on the 4th July the previous year and the whole of the United States had celebrated their marriage. Oh well, they'd got a year in, but I'd be really, really peeved at the world ending so close to the end of my walk.

In the morning, the world was still there and, as far as I could ascertain, going round, but it had all day to be cancelled yet.

Joyce and I walked to the station. Neither of us like prolonged partings, so we said goodbye and I walked on. I felt the emptiness you feel on such occasions, when you have just said goodbye to a good friend and it is prophesised that the world is about to end, but was distracted momentarily by meeting a lady who gave me a beaming smile and pressed Jehovah's Witness literature into my hands.

Today, I was headed for a camping site that was marked on my map, where I could find a corner to sleep, washing facilities and, most likely, a shop.

These were most beautiful lanes I walked along, with very, very steep hills, often wooded. I kept thinking how much Joyce would have loved the lanes but maybe not the hills quite so much. They were a bit serious.

There had been no traffic, but at East Tap house, I rejoined the A390 for a very nasty two and a half miles. I've got nothing against East Tap house, nor Middle Taphouse, nor West Taphouse. I passed through them all, as did the road and my sympathies are with all those taphouses. Then, I branched off on another delightful lane that Joyce would have loved, across Bofarnel Downs. It was very beautiful countryside and I came to a picnic spot that had an ice cream van waiting for me.

I stood on the bridge for a while, looking over it at the River Fowey racing along and then I walked down a manicured drive to Lanhydrock House.

The old house was well worth a visit. It was very impressive. The gatehouse alone, built in 1651 was like a castle, with its big arched gateway and turrets. A lot of the rest had burned down and been rebuilt in 1881, but the Long Gallery had not been burned and this had a fantastic ceiling, painted with scenes from the Old Testament.

Lanhydrock House is owned by the National Trust, which was fortunate because I could thus go in on my card without paying. It had 36 rooms open to the public. I left my rucksack at the entrance and whizzed around the House like an American tour of the planet. I could have easily spent a couple of days there, because it was so beautiful and there was such a lot of it, but I didn't think they would let me sleep in the House. I had actually enquired if there were "Volunteers" working there that week, because my card had been earned as a Volunteer and I was sure that I could muscle in with them for the night had there been a group, but they didn't know of any.

I had a stop in the café of course, for tea and cake, then filled my water bottle and went out into the gardens. They were beautiful too and I managed to cut through to the lane I needed, which saved a mile of walking.

I headed then to Lower Woon, where the camping site was marked as existing. Quite naturally, when I got there, a sign stated that no longer was there a camping site in that place and don't even think about it but then, very much to my surprise, I looked ahead and – there was a B

& B right in front of me.

As it had by then started raining, I had hopefully abandoned all plans for outside sleeping and knocked to see if there was room inside. Again to my surprise, there was. It looked as though life had become easier.

Doreen and Alan welcomed me and I soon settled in. It was just before sunset. Talking to Doreen, I learned that I was very close to the route of the Saints Way here. This old way crosses Cornwall from Padstow to Fowey, or even from Fowey to Padstow. I thought that, in the future, it would make a nice little circular walk to tread the coastal path from one of those towns and back across by the Saints Way. I put this in my mental filing cabinet, together with the B & B for such a future time.

In the morning, it was all right. Old Nostrus had been wrong. The planet was still rolling along in its gravitational well, the birds were singing and I was happy.

It was King Arthur's country around here. Or so they say. They also say it about Glastonbury, Wales and, even on the borders of the 'disputed lands' way up in the North, I had been assured that it was definitely there that he used to hang out.

I think the most likely one of the lot is Tintagel because once, years ago, I was there and had seen it with my own eyes - King Arthur's Car Park. I had not seen anywhere he could have parked his car in the other places, so this one must have been 'it'.

Cornwall has got loads of saints too. This Saints

Way I was near was really originally a track for traders in Bronze and Iron Age times but, much later, Celtic Christians used it and built churches, holy wells and those lovely granite crosses along the way.

I had noticed these crosses. At many crossroads, they were there. Some of them were only stubs now and looked like they'd been there a long, long time. Some were still proud and Celtic in their entirety, outlined against the sky. I thought they were very beautiful and impressive.

These saints did amazing things in their time. St Ia crossed the Irish Sea on an oak leaf, St. Illick sailed on a harrow and St. Petroc in a silver bowl. Most people used boats.

St. Samson was an important guy, who slew a serpent, raised the dead and converted pagans as he went along. I wondered if he knew St. Columb. They could have chatted for a long time about the relative sizes of the Loch Ness Monster and Cornish Serpents.

These little roads were very quiet. That morning, as I walked along them, only two cars came by me. Amazingly enough, they both came together, timing it so that they squeezed past each other at exactly the place where I was walking, so that I had to dive rather quickly into the hedge, thus receiving a stinging nettle up my trousers. What were the odds against that happening – the cars I mean, not the stinging nettle and were they blind drivers, not seeing me, or just stupid?

As I went along, I didn't feel too good and realised I'd caught what Joyce had been suffering from. I reckoned from the time that she had started feeling off colour and then it manifesting in my body, that she'd picked up a bug on the train coming out. It seemed to have roughly a three-day incubation time for the next person to get it. I think I had been brewing up a bit for it the previous day, but not enough to worry about at the time.

As the day got on, I felt worse and weak, having to make many trips to bushes. Then, I hit on a good idea. It was obviously some sort of bug in the gut. I had iodine drops with me and they killed bacteria and amoeba in water didn't they? Therefore, they would kill any nasties in my innards. After I was cured, I could eat some live yoghurt to replace the good and helpful bugs that live there normally.

So, I drank some water heavily laced with iodine.

(Caution! Please don't try this experiment at home. Please don't let any doctors read this.)

Well – it worked. I didn't feel too great, probably suffering now from iodine poisoning, but the bug slowly gave up on me.

I was going through a mining area now, where china clay was being dug out. It was a fascinating landscape, as I skirted St.Dennis and St.Stephen.

Saints everywhere! 174 parishes in Cornwall are dedicated to Saints.

The land I was walking through now might not

have appealed to tourists so much, but it was certainly interesting and different. Heaps of glistening white were all around me and I could see for a long way.

Despite not feeling too good, I was going well and aiming for Truro. I was only four miles short of my destination, when an amazing event happened.

There was blue sky on my left, blue sky on my right, blue sky in front, blue sky above. But behind me, creeping up unnoticed, was a long and black – very black, cloud. This cloud came over me and dropped its load. It continued to drop it for almost an hour. I was walking on an exposed lane, with nowhere to shelter and the rain falling was the same as if I'd been standing under a shower that was full on, or a small waterfall.

As I could see blue sky in the distance all around, this treatment felt as if it was deliberate and personal. Some malignant entity was saying to itself, "Ha! Only three days walking to go eh? Sent your spare trainers home have you? Thought the others would stay dry did you? You're usually a pessimist, what on earth made you start being an optimist? That will teach you!"

The road became a river and the water reached in places up to my ankles. Once, I saw a hedge and tried to shelter, but it was so saturated that there was no comfort there.

I was not pleased. It seemed downright unkind.

I waded down the road and saw a B & B sign. I knocked and a lady answered but said they were full. She was nice and invited me in out of the rain, but I didn't want to leave a pool on   her nice polished floor, so said I'd shelter for a while in the wood shed, if that was OK.

She said there was another B & B a short way ahead at St.Erme (another saint) and she'd be happy to phone and see if there was room. She did and there was. She told them I'd be there soon, so I thanked her for her kindness and bustled along.

The rain had almost stopped when I got there and I saw the fish sign on the door.

Dennis and Christine there were Pastors in the Pentecostal Church and, although I confessed to being more in the heathen line, it didn't make any difference to them, for I was made just as welcome as if I had been one of the Cornish Saints dropping in.

I didn't actually drop in, I dripped in. It had, I think, been the worst sudden downpour of the whole walk and that was saying something. They put my shoes in a room near a machine that took moisture out of the air and the other clothes were soon dried.

Dennis and Christine had been missionaries in Uganda, India and Romania and, from listening to them, I found that they were respectful of the peoples' way of lives in those places and had really roughed it at times, but with enthusiasm, spirit and always a good sense of humour. Once, Christine said, when in Africa, she had been ill and discovered that a 'hex' had been put on her. They had always thought that such a thing only worked if you knew you had been cursed and believed in it. Here though, she had not even known that it had been done and certainly did not believe in the power of such a thing, but still, it had caused trouble. The hex had to be taken off by using the correct rituals, then it was OK. That makes you think.

It was very interesting to me, hearing of their amazingly strong faith and how it always seemed to work. Dennis seemed to be able to listen to God and chat to him on everyday terms and their accounts of the times this had proved effective were fascinating and impressive.

An example was that they had known they should buy a house and settle for a while, but not known where. It could have been anywhere in the country, but auction details of this one had come to their notice and God had told Dennis to go and bid for it.

So they went to the auction and put in a bid. He said that God had assured him he'd get it for a certain amount, but after that sum had been reached, the price kept going up.

"Hold on," Dennis had said in his head to God, "You said we'd get the house for less than that."

"Carry on," God had said. "Don't worry about it, it's OK." So, in complete faith, Dennis did carry on bidding, but the price went £20,000 over the amount they had available.

They got the house and had managed to borrow the extra from an Aunt, but hated having to do this. Shortly afterwards though, when they'd moved in, they discovered that a piece of land beyond the hedge at the bottom of the garden, belonged to them too. They had had no idea of this. They sold the land for £25,000, which repaid the loan and legal costs.

"Well, God said it would be all right," said Dennis. "And it was."

Another time, they got the message to go to India – "Just go!" So they did, paying by credit card because they didn't have the money available. When over there, they went out for a walk and, by chance, wandered into Mother Theresa's orphanage, where they stayed helping, for half a year. When they got back, they had expected there to be this enormous amount owing for the airline fare and waiting to be paid, plus interest on the card, but there was nothing. They had been the millionth booking on that airline and the prize for that had been free transport.

"You see," laughed Dennis. "God is up to date – he's not above using credit cards."

There were many other tales of such faith from those lovely people. They were not trying to convert me, I felt accepted as I was, but I did find our talk together very interesting. It seemed to me they had great courage as well as faith. Any money they had left after paying their bills, they gave to somebody who needed it and they said, always, they had enough for the next lot of bills.

Off I went the next day, with shoes pretty nearly dry and feeling good. I had quaffed more iodine and it seemed OK, so I thought that was probably the end of the bug. Poor little devil, cut off in its prime, but my insides were not its home. It had been an unwelcome squatter.

The main road to Truro I had to follow was busy and unpleasant for two miles then fine, because I branched off on to a little road. As I got into town, I met Dennis and Christine driving out, having done their shopping. They had offered me a lift, but I wasn't going to cheat now.

Truro was a nice looking city. I walked alongside the Cathedral. People had been settled here for the last 2,500 years. I liked it a lot.

On the way out of Truro, I got chatting with a man who was walking my way and who asked in which direction I was heading. Then, having heard that bit of information, he very confidently assured me that I was going the wrong way.

I didn't think I was going the wrong way, but he was adamant. He was going a bit in the direction I wanted, he said and would show me the right way. So he took hold of my arm and marched me along, to make sure I didn't get lost. He had been living there for 20 years he said, so should know which direction it was and, so he should, but I didn't think he did, because we were now walking East and I wanted to go West. I had this modern contraption called a compass you see. Thank goodness, he left me to go wherever he was going, so I could wave a cheery goodbye and then turn and walk back again, without hurting his feelings.

After that, I found my way with no trouble and walked in deserted Cornish countryside where seemingly none of the tourists wished to go. It was lovely country too, sometimes like Sussex, sometimes like Devon but mostly, I suspect, like Cornwall.

Looking at my map, the names of the villages around this part were strange, but often happy sounding, like 'Playing Place', which sounded fun and a smaller one called 'Come to Good', which was tempting. Then, there was a cuddly little village called 'Hugus', after a visit to which a person would 'Gloweth' and could find that they had a 'Green Bottom'.

I met a gentleman called Peter, who was walking from Lands End to John O'Groats. He was hoping to do it in 8 weeks. We had a good chat. Peter had had a nervous breakdown and was hoping the walk would help to get him back to health. I hoped it would and thought so. I knew that all stresses had fallen away from me during the walk very quickly and that I had felt very good. It had made me appreciate the people I loved and I was very much looking forward to seeing them all. I had realised and valued the good things in my life.

Peter had left the cause of his stress, which was teaching. So many teachers seem to suffer from this now, which is sad. I was going back to my mother, who I loved very much indeed, but there was no doubt that it was a commitment that caused stress and I had left that stress behind me for a while. My walk had taught me that whether or not I felt guilty about the feeling, the result was the same – the stress was caused by doing something I didn't want to do. Much as I tried to tell myself I did want to do it because I loved my mother and it was the right thing to do, I could not convince the true person inside. Whether that inside person was good or selfish was immaterial – the result was how it was. Now I was on my way back to a way of life that I could not convince myself I liked much, I had found that the headaches were beginning again. Still, I was far from the only person in the world to be doing something I did not want to do and not many could have had the time to do the walk I'd almost done now. I had been a lucky one, who had managed to fulfil at least one dream.

I enjoyed my chat with Peter, who was a very pleasant man. He told me that there had been no rain where he was walking the previous day and could hardly believe my tales of the personalised downpour. He told me that he'd stayed the previous night at 'The Star' in Porkellis and that the people there had been lovely. He had aimed to camp along the way but, having done that the first night, thought B & Bs were much more comfortable. I sympathised with that.

I came to Stithians Reservoir, which was a large expanse of water, popular with people. I crossed just a narrow part of it, most of the water being on my left, over the fields, where I caught glimpses of it glistening for a long way. There were lots of birds around and I learned afterwards that it is a popular place for birdwatchers.

It was just the right temperature for walking, not too hot, cloudy but with no rain. I kept getting a bit nervous though, whenever I saw what I thought might be an extra blackish cloud approaching, but it was OK. As soon as I got to a phone box, I phoned The Star and managed to book a place, so even though it had been quite a long way that day, I could really enjoy the final two miles.

As I walked, I had noticed that the plants around me were often verging on 'exotic'. It was like I was walking somewhere in a Mediterranean country rather than England. I actually saw Kangaroo Paw growing in a garden. I had only ever seen that in Australia before.

It was true what Peter had told me. John and Sandy at The Star were lovely. It felt like I had become one of their family for a while. Their daughter Jane was practising for the Carnival, dressed as one of the 'Men in Black'. She worked at the nearby Poldark Mine. I had heard of that. It was an old tin mine, but done up for tourists now, where they can experience a bit of what it used to be like.

There had been so many things, like that mine, I should have liked to visit in more detail. My walk had been a 'taster' of places I should like to return to and explore, but if I had stopped for them all, I should not be half way along my walk and my sister would surely go insane. And what about the parts of the country I had not even gone near? There were certainly enough places in Great Britain to occupy me for the rest of my life.

I wondered just how long I had. Would I live to the full 90 years my mother had reached, or would she outlive me? The other year my sister had almost beaten her to it with ovarian cancer. The cancer was caught just in time, because the surgeon said that if the diagnosis had been a month later, it would have been 'curtains' for her, but now she had passed all the tests so far.

That had been a bad year. A couple of months before that, my daughter had leaned on a china sink, which had been cracked and her arm had gone right through, severing 10 of the tendons in her wrist, the muscle and artery. Her hand had fortunately fallen at an angle that blocked off the flow of blood, or she would be gone too. The people who operated on her at Exeter hospital and those who worked on it at East Grinstead Queen Victoria, made her hand work pretty near normally again.

There had been a lot of other stresses that year too. It goes like that but, at the end of it all, on Christmas Day, I sat amongst my loved ones. I looked at Heather and Anne laughing together and, everything seemed very good. Nothing else mattered. Either one or both of them could have been dead, but here they were, alive and laughing. I had felt so very happy. When I get 'down' I think of that sometimes, how it could have been and yet, how it was. It was probably because I was in such a family atmosphere and almost home that I had thought about them all that evening.

I really enjoyed my stay with that lovely family at 'The Star'. Sandy waved me off the next day. It was a walk of around 15 miles to go I reckoned because, I was going to try to get to Penzance and stay there for two nights. That would mean that I could walk to Lands End the final day, light of heart and light of foot – without my rucksack.

It was a good walk and now, I must have been in popular walking country, for I started to meet ramblers and people on holiday.

I came to Godolphin Cross, which has Godolphin House nearby. That is Tudor and Elizabethan, built with mining money and apparently sitting in deep woodland. I was very tempted to go there but, with the end of my walk the next day and a long way to go, I decided it would be another thing that I might do in the future.

The name Marazion had for some reason intrigued me. As I reached it, I couldn't believe the most beautiful gardens and hanging baskets, full of colour and splendour that were lighting up even the most humble of houses and shops. There was a competition shortly for the most beautiful place and Marazion was assuredly trying hard. I thought it was so very lovely and hoped for their success in the judgement.

I walked along the coast at Marazion and, into view, came St. Michaels Mount. It was beautiful and mysterious, this mount. The tide was in, so it was cut off from the land but, when the tide is out, you can walk across the causeway. Mike and me had done that many, many years ago, way back in 1960 but not here. We had walked across to its sister (or brother?) in France so, looking at the English version brought back a lot of memories.

Marazion probably got its name from the bit of water between it and the Mount because Mara means Sea and Zion small, so the whole meaning is small sea.

Someone told me that, hundreds of years ago, some locals saw a vision of the Archangel Michael above the wooded mount, so a monastery was built there in his name.

The island is made of granite and is 300 feet high, so with the monastery and castle on top of that, it is a magical sight. Lots of stories of King Arthur are associated with it of course, because he got everywhere, but I couldn't see where he could have parked his car.

I managed to get Mike on the phone and was pleased, because I could tell him that I was looking at St. Michael's Mount while I was talking to him and that was quite a boast, it being so near the end of the walk. He sounded proud of me that I was almost there.

Needless to say, I had a cup of tea and as large a slice of cake as I could get my hands on and my mouth around – and that's pretty large. Then, I toddled the rest of the way into Penzance, as happy as anything.

The final bit wasn't going to provide easy-to-get accommodation there because it was July now, well into the holiday season. I wanted to get accommodation on this last time so that I could leave the rucksack. I called at seven B & Bs, but none had room, or if they did, it was for two people and they wouldn't let to just one.

Sometimes it seems as if civilisation and, most probably nature, abhors a single unit. Circumstances and people always seem to favour a couple. Noah wouldn't even have taken me on board the Ark and it was certainly more expensive being a lone person.

All contact with people running B & Bs and cafes

in Cornwall so far had not seemed to be Cornish people. It seemed that most of the places were run by those who had loved Cornwall and come into it seeking to stay and earn a living there. Talking to a local person, they said that there was not very good local feeling about that sometimes, because it had forced the prices of the property up for the ones already there and most of the money brought in by tourists did not benefit the native Cornwallians.

Finally, on my search for accommodation, I found Joyce, who only let out for part of the year and it ended up that I had found somewhere very good.

The room I had was really a double, but she didn't mind. It was reasonable in price and luxurious. Joyce did the decorating herself and was busy with some now. I liked her a lot.

It felt strange, as I put down my rucksack and gear, to know that I didn't have to bother to get myself prepared much any more. I wasn't even going to take that faithful old rucksack with me the next day.

I looked at my dear old trainers which, except when they had been soaking wet, I had worn all the time. They were not even worn out, just the start of holes forming on the soles. I vowed to take them back to the shop to show them and give praise. People mostly go back to complain, it would be good to express how satisfied I was.

Clean and glowing, I wandered out to look around Penzance a bit. First, I walked to the railway and coach station. Unusually, they were in the same place, not at opposite ends of the town, which is much more usual. After enquiring, there was no question about whether it should be train or coach going back home. The train cost £50 more, so it was definitely coach, which would get me to the station from where I could catch a train home and I didn't have to travel across London. So, even though it was longer sitting on the coach, there wasn't so much difference in the end. It took me a lot of hours to earn £50 from gardening work, so I didn't mind sitting on a coach for a few extra. Saving on spending the money is as good as earning it.

I sat on the front looking at the sea and eating a sandwich. There was a notice warning against feeding the seagulls. It said they were becoming aggressive and a nuisance because of people feeding them. Huh! I wasn't about to share my sandwich with a seagull anyway but, then, one came swooping down and landed on the arm of the seat by my side, eyeing up that sandwich.

It was a very big bird, but not as big as me. I caught its eye and we stared at each other.

"Forget it sunshine," I said. "Go and catch fish." It could see that it had met its match and flew off.

Then, I walked back through the Sub-Tropical Botanical Gardens and sat there a while. It was difficult to believe I was still in England, with these tropical plants all around me. One had flowers of an enormous height. I expected to see parakeets fly overhead and monkeys swinging in the undergrowth. It was balmy and warm too, so I stayed in those beautiful gardens, fascinated, until the sun was low. Then I went back to my lodgings.

Joyce was going off to the Minack Open Air Theatre that evening. I thought how nice it was that she felt at ease leaving me, a stranger, in her house. I sat and watched the television for a while and that night, had a very sound sleep.

Next day, 8th July, was the day! There was a beautiful blue sky, suitable for the occasion.

THE LAST LEG

It was such a happy day, with the sun beating down and a load-free walk of only about 11 miles, with plenty of time to do it in.

I chose to walk inland, because I intended to walk the Coastal Path another time, so cut off at Newlyn, taking the smallest roads I could.

There was a point, when I was on a track and in some woods, that gave me a most pleasant feeling. The woods were ancient, with the sun dappling moss-covered stones. There were lichens hanging from the trees and, as I sat in them for a while, I felt very much at home. Somehow it felt as if I knew them and they knew me. It strengthened my determination to return to this strange, yet very familiar part of the country.

I passed through St. Buryan, where there were two very big megaliths called 'The Pipers'. They were erected by King Athelstan to celebrate his victory of the last official punch-up between the Cornish and the English, in AD935. The stones were put there to seal the treaty. They must have had to use an enormous lump of sealing wax.

Over the road were 19 stones, called the Merry Maidens. I was told there were 19 anyway. I didn't go and check on them for myself. They were still made use of at gatherings, when new bards were admitted to the Goredd – College of Bards.

Lots of ancient stones and sites remain undisturbed in Cornwall. That is because it is pretty much an island, what with the River Tamar dividing it from Devon. With dangerous roads and dubious sea travel, for a long time, it was left alone. It firmed my opinion that, originally, these stones were everywhere, making up the matrix of everyday life. Another plan came into my mind that I could come back to Cornwall and visit all the ancient sites I could find, just for the hell of it.

I walked then, down and down, through a place very aptly named 'Bottoms', then, coming out on to the B3315, cut off down a track towards the sea.

It was easy to find the way, because the sea was pretty big to aim for, so I came out onto the Coastal Path. Then, I got a bit mislaid around an inlet where it was hard to see where to go, but rejoined the path again and it was beautiful.

This was a rugged coast of cliffs, rocks and sparkling blue sea. I was seeing it behaving its very best on this glorious summer day.

I was soon to be arriving at Land's End. It could have been that I would have had friends there to meet me.

The previous year, I had met Norah and Bill on an overnight stay in a B & B. They were true Cornish people and lived at Hayle, not far away. Without even knowing me, I had been invited to stay with them for the total eclipse of the sun, which I later did and, although the eclipse was clouded out and it rained, it was a most happy and delightful time spent with them.

Bill is 80 and is well known for his involvement in promoting running locally and runs regularly himself, taking part in the London Marathon every year and once, in the New York Marathon. He started all this running quite late in life and it suits him well, for I should like to be like him when I'm 80.

Norah was also mature when she took up art and I was very impressed by the beautiful pastels and paintings I saw on the walls. They were very good and it is a shame that she suffers too much now from muscle fatigue to be able to paint, because she has a real talent.

I had felt so very warmed by the generosity and welcome of this lovely couple to somebody who was a complete stranger, but is one no longer.

I had arranged to phone Norah and Bill when I was near them and would have then walked through Hayle and stayed with them. I knew they were most likely on holiday in early July, but had not thought for one moment that I would be down in Cornwall by that time. So, making good time as I had, they were away when I arrived, which disappointed them (and me). They had aimed to be at Land's End to welcome and congratulate me when I walked in.

So, I walked into the complex at Lands End by myself, without any trumpets or fanfare – not even a rucksack on my back to indicate that I had done the walk.

It would have been lovely to have seen Norah and Bill and part of me would have liked to have been met with a big cheer and waving of flags, but the other part didn't expect it to matter to anybody else and didn't really believe it was such a big deal anyway.

It had been a walk. An ambition and not so hard as all that. I accepted the doing of it and the finish as something done now and felt neither strong elation, nor an anticlimax, only happiness and pleasure at the end of something achieved, the pleasant day's walk I had just had and the sun.

I did go and sign the register. The lady in charge of it was so sweet. She made me feel that I was special and shook my hand in congratulation, even though it was a regular happening.

I had a large ice-cream then and became a tourist. I had to have a photo taken of me in front of the signpost at the 'end' of course and had saved the last two photos on my final disposable camera for this purpose. I asked one of the people standing around if they would take a couple of photos, explaining proudly that I'd just finished the walk, but they looked at me sideways, doubtfully. They took my picture though. It would have cost serious money to have had one taken officially inside the enclosure and to get close to the sign, you had to pay that, which I thought was a rip-off so wasn't having any. I didn't have to prove to anybody that I had done the walk anyway.

There was an old fishing boat dry-docked there that people could go on. I did and immediately felt a very strange sensation of familiarity and the sensation was just as though the boat was moving, although it most certainly was not. As I walked along the deck, it felt as though it was undulating with the waves and, when I stepped off, the ground was firm and different under my feet. I felt a bit strange for a while. I was obviously on a slightly different planet but it felt great.

There was an announcement over speakers that a young man who had cycled the length for charity was just about to arrive and it would be nice to welcome him in. So, I joined the small crowd that gathered to cheer the young man as he arrived.

He cycled in, looking fit and sun-tanned, with clear complexion and grinning happily. He had not expected such a welcome. His parents stood there proudly, collecting any further contributions for the charity he had been cycling for. He had cause to be proud and so had they. I gave them the amount that I could have wasted on an unnecessary photo and it made me feel good, like a celebration of my own walk.

I enjoyed myself as a tourist and, when I had had enough, took an open-top bus back to St.Just, where I changed for Penzance.

I saved the bus driver's sanity. He had been under constant bombardment on the way down by a Japanese lady who could not speak very much English but who was very worried about where to get off, then, when to get on again. He had helped all he could and breathed a sign of relief when she left but now, he had just seen her approaching the bus for the return trip.

This lady was going to Penzance, so I said I'd stick with her and help. The driver almost threw his arms around me.

The Japanese lady was very pleasant, when parted from the insecurity of finding her way and we had a good trip back together to Penzance, managing to communicate satisfactorily.

It felt very odd being on a bus and knowing I was not going to walk the next day.

On the morrow, it felt even stranger, sitting down in the coach for all that way and taking only hours for what would have taken me a long time to walk.

I walked from the Station at East Grinstead. It was about a mile to home. My sister had asked if I wanted a lift when I got to the station, but I had said, "Don't be silly," and walked.

I arrived home and there were paper letters strung up saying "Welcome Home Pat". Anne had arranged just a small party the next day for family, Joyce and Chris, another friend. I was very loved and it felt good. Mum was very pleased to see me. I wasn't sure if she realised how far I had walked, but I was completely sure of her welcome.

The strange thing was, I didn't feel like it had been a linear time away at all. It felt like I had been in a bubble of time and space growing out sideways, separate from the normal flow of past to future.

Now, time was joined up again and the walk was in that bubble, contained in it for me to look at whenever I felt like it.

And so I would. When I am an old, old woman and not able to walk like that anymore, I shall go into that bubble sometimes and see the places and people again.

* * *

Every night, for a whole month, I dreamed that I was walking.

* * *

Printed in Great Britain
by Amazon